SET FOR INCLUSION

SET FOR INCLUSION

An Underlying Methodology for Achieving Your Inclusion Dividend

MASON DONOVAN

MARK KAPLAN

First published by Bibliomotion, Inc.
39 Harvard Street
Brookline, MA 02445
Tel: 617-934-2427
www.bibliomotion.com

Printed in the United States of America

Library of Congress Cataloging-in-Publication Data

Donovan, Mason.
SET for inclusion : an underlying methodology for achieving your inclusion dividend / Mason Donovan, Mark Kaplan.
pages cm
ISBN 978-1-62956-082-3 (hardcover : alk. paper) — ISBN 978-1-62956-083-0 (ebook)
1. Diversity in the workplace. 2. Corporate culture. 3. Management—Cross-cultural studies. I. Kaplan, Mark (Human resources consultant) II. Title.
HF5549.5.M5D663 2015
658.3008—dc23

2015008550

In Loving Memory of
Doris Jean "DJ" Kaplan
1942–2014

A woman who valued lifelong education
and the pursuit of inclusion.

Contents

Foreword

Diversity means business, but not without inclusion...

The financial and organizational benefits of a diverse workforce are now so well established and discussed that—at least for the most part—everyone "gets it."

However, I think the more difficult question is, when can an organization deem their diversity efforts a success? Is it when you look the way you would hope in terms of reflecting your customers, clients, shareholders, and communities?

The answer, of course, is no. You're not done. An organization can have no real success with diversity, without inclusion.

I have found that there is no magic formula to achieving inclusion in the workplace because often times, people who are not inclusive are not doing it on purpose. They're doing what's comfortable—going to people like them, with similar backgrounds, thoughts, and values. But that approach does not offer perspective, and it alienates members of the team.

Business leaders recognize this, but they also don't have time for the complicated adjustments, they need someone to tell them what's wrong and how to fix it.

That is why I appreciate the SET model. It's simple and impactful by providing a strategy to develop inclusive leaders who build inclusive teams, and hold employees accountable. True inclusion may take time to achieve but to achieve it—or at a minimum improve—will transform your organization and bottom line.

I anticipate you're reaching for this book in the search for a methodology that will help you tackle the inclusion opportunity in your organization. As the authors point out, while this book won't give you every answer you seek, it will give you a way to know where to look. It all starts with a strong culture, and leaders focused on providing an inclusive environment.

I hope you enjoy the book and the model as much as I have.

Michelle Fullerton,
Diversity and Inclusion Executive
Financial Services

Preface

There are three core types of diversity and inclusion consultancies: 1) activist consultants working for civil change, 2) academic consultants who lecture on theory and philosophy, and 3) corporate consultants who are firmly based in the business case. We, The Dagoba Group, are decidedly a corporate diversity and inclusion (D&I) firm. We believe development should be practical, be immediately applicable, and provide a measurable return. Our work is steeped in the business case, and we see diversity and inclusion as a business investment. Awareness is necessary but not sufficient. Today's D&I conversation needs to focus on practical application with short- and long-term impact.

Between the two of us, we—your authors—have read hundreds of business-related books. Over the past twenty-some years of developing leaders in the field of diversity and inclusion, we have consumed dozens of books focused specifically on D&I. We would go through the same process with every book, reading the first twenty or so pages to determine whether the book was written for us or for the purpose we were seeking. Some were written specifically for diversity practitioners while others were general in nature. We all have a finite amount of time to devote to reading, so let us make the choice easier for you. Rather than expecting you to sift through the next chapter to decide if this book is for you, we want to give you insight up front.

Let's first say who will not find great value in this book. If you are an academic looking for research on D&I for your next paper, this book will not help you achieve that goal. If you are an activist seeking educational leverage to change legislation, we regret to inform you that this is most likely not your book. Although both researchers and activists make valuable contributions to D&I, this book is really written for those in the corporate world.

SET for Inclusion is targeted to business leaders and corporate leadership development teams alike. Many of you may have attended a Dagoba workshop or participated in one of our e-learning programs. If you have, this book will help you refresh and supplement your learning experience. Some of you may not have had the opportunity to attend a workshop, but want to see the method thousands of global leaders are leveraging to create more inclusive workplaces. If you are a business leader, you will gain practical insight with application at the C-suite, management, and individual contributor level. Our targeted reader wants to create a stronger, more inclusive team environment to help move the organization forward. Much like *The Inclusion Dividend*, this book is written in an easy-to-read style with stories that resonate. As a D&I practitioner, you will discover important insights and learn how to implement them with a very practical approach.

Although this book supplements the best-selling D&I book *The Inclusion Dividend: Why Investing in Diversity and Inclusion Pays Off*, you do not have to read that book first.

When we touch upon inclusion concepts, we will provide some overview and will point you back to *The Inclusion Dividend* if you want a deeper dive. *SET for Inclusion* is about how to apply D&I concepts in an everyday work environment where you have many competing priorities. It allows you to realize you do not have to move mountains in order to experience a difference. We focus on the small, practical actions you can influence. The goal of this book is to allow you to easily integrate into your everyday decision making those sometimes complex inclusion concepts you have been struggling to implement.

Acknowledgments

This book is the embodiment of an inclusion dividend. Our exposure to a diverse group of clients, colleagues, and mentors has helped us to craft what we believe to be a simple, but yet powerful model. There are far too many individuals to thank, so let's focus on the teams. We are grateful to the Bibliomotion team that has assisted us in refining the story and providing the seamless support to publish a quality read. Appreciation and respect go out to our group of global consultants who not only provided us valuable feedback on how the model was resonating, but also facilitated an impactful experience for our clients. A resounding level of applause to our clients who realize the value of inclusion and thus invest the time and resources to develop tens of thousands of leaders every year; we would not be here without you. Of course our arms are wide open to our family and friends, who understood how our free time was limited by writing deadlines, but were also there to act as a sounding board. Lastly, we want to thank everyone who has attended our workshops and openly shared their challenges while committing to creating a truer meritocracy for all.

Introduction to the SET Model

> There is nothing like returning to a place that remains unchanged to find the ways in which you yourself have altered.
>
> —*Nelson Mandela*

At one time or another, we have all been to an amazing workshop. The instructor started off with a great premise that fit a current challenge we were facing. She was charismatic. The "ahas" were audible around the room. The model presented at the onset was simple. "I can do this," you told yourself. Maybe it was based on three pillars. "Yes, yes, it all makes sense." You learned that the first knowledge pillar rests on four supporting platforms; that's a little more complicated, but it made sense. Further into the workshop, you discovered that each platform is made up of three layers of wisdom, which each connect in some way to five truths. You took copious notes as you told yourself this was really going to help you tackle that pressing work challenge. Before you knew it, the six-hour workshop was over. You were engaged throughout. Eagerly toting the glossy, very organized three-ring presentation binder you had filled with notes, you thanked the instructor and the organizer. "This has really helped me," you said earnestly. You placed the binder on the side of your desk, intending to apply the knowledge soon; not now, though, because you first had to get through some e-mails and prepare for the next day's client call. A few days passed, jam-packed with meetings. The binder was moved over to your bookshelf to make way for the quarterly reports.

A week later, you were in a team meeting where that challenge-the one you took the workshop to solve—surfaced again. "Ah, I am glad you asked that question, as I was just in a great training about this," you told your colleagues excitedly. "First, we need to establish the primary pillar," you lectured as you turned to the whiteboard. You sounded brilliant. You drew the pillar on the board. "Before we can apply this pillar we need to understand it is supported by..." you stopped to scratch your head to wrangle that information. You regained your thought process, "by three or four platforms, I think she called it." You could remember two of the platforms. You then drew two more figures under that to symbolize the layers and truths, but were not sure which were which. "It all seemed so simple in the class," you mumbled. "You know what, let me get back to that when I have more time to review my notes," you tell your colleagues. If this has happened to you, you are not alone. Competing research varies as to the amount of learning we retain, but all studies agree it is nowhere close to 100 percent.

A year later, your office space is being renovated so you are boxing up items for temporary storage. You pull the binder from the shelf, dust it, and flip through its pages.

You read a few of your scribbled notes, but they don't make much sense to you anymore. The binder does not fit into your box, so you put it in the recycle pile. The original challenge remains unmoved, but you promise yourself you will get to it after the annual reviews.

Why are we starting off with this story? To be candid, the problem of content retention and application is what propelled us to create the SET methodology a few years ago. Diversity and inclusion are about human behavior and interaction. Everyone from academics to seasoned consultants like ourselves were doing their best to help organizations build more inclusive cultures. Like many in the D&I field, we had created presentations that featured concentric circles, pillars, and every type of PowerPoint SmartArt flow-chart shape you can think of to help us explain how to move from point A to point B.

There were many "aha" moments when participants really connected and absorbed the learning objectives. "We made a difference," we would tell ourselves. The workshop scores were great. However, every now and then we would bump into former workshop participants and ask them how they were doing. They would genuinely enthuse about how great the workshop was, but then a certain look would fall upon their faces, as if they were embarrassed about something. Inevitably, they would say they had not accomplished their goals and probably should take the workshop again. And they often asked for a book that explained the concepts in a straightforward way. Out of that request came *The Inclusion Dividend: Why Investing in Diversity and Inclusion Pays Off.* We wrote that book because we could not find a book that was written for the everyday business leader who wanted to foster a diverse and inclusive workplace but did not have a firm knowledge of D&I concepts. There were plenty of books for D&I practitioners; however, these books were not written for business leaders and they did not speak to the needs of businesspeople. Given that corporations are investing approximately $8 billion globally on diversity and inclusion, there needed to be a more tangible return, something that had a measurable impact upon the company's success.

Concept Development Strategy

The Inclusion Dividend was part of the Dagoba strategy to do two things: first, to bring D&I from the academic world into the workplace, and second, to move beyond awareness and toward measureable practical application. So we went to work, distilling twenty-plus years of experience and knowledge into an easily digestible written format.

We knew, however, that the book would take a couple of years to write and publish. We wanted to make a difference immediately and we knew it had to start in the classroom. All of the models, figures, and shapes made perfect sense to us and to our fellow consultants, but we were not our target audience. It is a typical mishap in educational workshops that the facilitators create programs that fit themselves better than they fit the learner. Our two-pronged goal: make our model memorable and make it practical. After a few hours of trying to flatten or simplify our existing models, we realized that we had to ditch all of them and start from scratch.

Before we started, we tested on colleagues and clients the number of ideas we could realistically expect a participant to remember one week after a workshop. The answer was three.

Three seemed to be a very common number, both in and out of the workplace, when it came to knowledge as well as memory. Okay, we had our foundation. Three things. Even with three items, we could easily complicate the model, as we showed in the story at the start of this introduction. The three things could not rest on a multitude of other items that people needed to remember, or the model would not work.

So if we wanted participants to remember three things, what was the one challenge we were trying to accomplish with these three things? We charted a list of ideas, from building a diverse pipeline to managing team dynamics to creating a culture of inclusion. There were far too many "walk aways" that were important, and that was the crux of the problem. We walked away and let it rest for a while. The next day, as we were cleaning up the flip-chart paper we'd tossed onto the floor so that we could brainstorm for an upcoming client meeting, the solution struck us. We realized that the lists of "walk aways" strewn about the floor really boiled down to one thing. We knew leaders were going to be presented with big challenges, and in some of these challenges inclusion had a heavy influence while in others it had a small role. We could not try to arm leaders with information on dealing with each and every challenge they might face, but we could give them a common tool for managing any challenge.

The one challenge we needed to address was how to integrate inclusion into the decision-making process. When you boil away all of the theory about D&I, at some level the turning point always comes down to decisions being made by individuals, particularly leaders, that determine the inclusivity of an outcome. With a simple tool that focused on decision making, regardless of the challenge, leaders could approach the issue in the same manner every time.

If, for example, you are presented with a decision that involves people, and which would benefit from being viewed through a lens of inclusion, what are the three things you need to do? First, you need to recognize that the situation involves inclusion, directly or indirectly, and identify your starting point coming into this decision. We call that first step of our model *Self-Awareness*. You might think of this as going from *not knowing* what you don't know to *knowing* what you don't know. Awareness is great, and in fact is necessary, but it's not sufficient if you are going to solve a problem, so we knew you had to leverage this awareness by thinking about the situation differently. We didn't want leaders to go backward from the dissonance created by self-awareness. To put this thought in other words, becoming aware that your behaviors are the barriers to inclusion may cause you to stop listening if you are not given a pathway to correct them. Who wants to know what is wrong if you have no way to fix it? Once you are fully aware, it is time to move to the next stage. This stage of the process we call *Engage System 2*. Don't worry about what that means at this point; we will go through it in detail in chapter 2. At its core, Engage System 2 is about interrupting our existing thought process to allow new behavior to emerge. At this step in the model you have heightened awareness of the situation and your starting point and you are able to apply a different way of thinking about it. If you walk away now, is anything solved? While you are closer to a solution, the answer is no. The only thing you have done up to this point is educate yourself and start a new way of thinking; nothing was actually done.

The last stage is vital; you need to take action based on these first two steps. This last step we call *Tailor.* Now, don't let us fool you into thinking these words just flowed onto the paper and surreptitiously spelled out SET. We began with concepts and distilled them into words, which we then manipulated to form a very simple, easy-to-remember word. Luckily, it was a word that was easily applied to different phrases, such as *SET for Inclusion.* We actually started with the familiar phrase "Ready, SET, Go," but it felt too unfocused for our work.

The very first time we brought the SET decision-making methodology into a classroom, it was a resounding success. The true test came four weeks later when we met with the same group again. We asked them to write down one or two things they remembered about the workshop. More than 90 percent of participants wrote down SET as one of their two things, and 100 percent of them had remembered something useful. We hit one of our goals: make it memorable. But was it practical? One of the participants not only had written "SET" as one of her points, she also went into how she applied the concept successfully one week after the workshop. Memorable *and* practical! We'd accomplished the learning goals while helping others turn their "aha" moments into action.

Though *The Inclusion Dividend* book was still in the formative stages at that time, we knew that with our SET model we could immediately begin to disrupt the industry's thought process when it came to integrating inclusion into everyday workplace decisions. Although we develop thousands of leaders globally every year, reaching a far wider audience required a book that could distribute the knowledge further. We are proud to say *The Inclusion Dividend* hit the target square on, proving a great success at helping leaders who are not D&I practitioners fully comprehend the benefits of a diverse and inclusive workplace. The strategy all along was to supplement the base of knowledge featured in *The Inclusion Dividend* with the SET decision-making methodology. In this book, so as not to reinvent the wheel, we will not speak in depth to the underlying diversity and inclusion concepts that we devote chapters to in *The Inclusion Dividend.* Instead, we will refer you to that book to gain a more in-depth understanding of the concepts. *SET for Inclusion* is intended to help those who need a simple and yet practical approach to decision making for inclusion.

Meet Our Colleagues

To help bring the points to life, we are going to follow three individuals who, like most, are well intentioned when it comes to diversity and inclusion but are finding it difficult to match their results with their intent. Although the individuals and the company they work for are fictionalized, we believe you will find them familiar. Indeed, they are composites of many individuals we have worked with over the years, though they do not represent any particular individual or company. Let's meet the three colleagues.

Jameson is the new CEO of VeStrong, a company born of a recent merger of global insurance company All Vector Insurance and financial management firm Strong Choice Investments Inc. VeStrong is a leader in life insurance and retirement planning. The press called the joining of the two firms a merger, but really it was an acquisition. Jameson and his executive team were members of the former insurance company, All Vector, and they took on all of the executive management roles in the new firm. The board members were drawn evenly from the boards of both companies.

Now for a little personal data about Jameson. Jameson is white and recently celebrated his fifty-seventh birthday. He grew up in a solidly middle-class white neighborhood in the suburbs of Boston, married his high school sweetheart, and eventually had three children. He was a proud graduate of Boston University, and often asked specifically for BU students to fill his internships. His wife was a work-at-home mom and frequently attended Jameson's work social events. She'd formed friendships with many of Jameson's executive team and their spouses. Overall, Jameson felt his executive team had a really good bond.

Jameson's very public diversity and inclusion challenge came just weeks after he took the helm as CEO. After a series of layoffs due to acquisition redundancies, local news picked up on the demographics of those who were being released. The layoffs were hitting a particularly disproportionate percentage of minorities. In addition, the newspaper ran an editorial that highlighted the fact that the diverse management team of acquired Strong Choice Investment was replaced by Jameson's team of all white middle-aged men. The article pointed to several Catalyst global studies from 2004 to 2011 that found a diverse management team resulted in anywhere from 16 percent to 30 percent better return on equity. Two large institutional clients sent Jameson letters of concern. In addition, a highly visible RFP (request for proposal) had been reissued with a much more detailed questionnaire on VeStrong's diversity and inclusion practices.

Jameson thought he could easily explain all of the issues.

First, the layoffs were simply based on redundant offices that were closing due to the merger. Most of these offices were formerly Strong Choice Investments (SCI). SCI had initiated a successful diversity recruitment program, and this, together with the company's broad demographic market reach, was one of the primary reasons future investors gave for increasing SCI's market value. Second, Jameson thought he'd picked the best management team to run the new business. During the negotiation, he noticed that SCI's management team had too many personalities in the mix and relied heavily on consensus decision making. He felt that decisiveness and the ability to take quick action were important in the new company. In fact, some key investors had said as much, and they pointed out that the value proposition for the merger depended upon quick action. The diversity of the team didn't even cross Jameson's mind. It wasn't a factor. He told one of the investors it did not matter to him what color or gender the people on his team were. He only wanted the best, and his existing team was the best.

As for the client letters and the reissued RFP, Jameson knew something had to be done, if only to prevent the appearance that the company was discriminating in any way. He asked his assistant, Betty, to schedule a meeting with Libby. Libby had been with All Vector Insurance for almost fifteen years, and was sales manager for one of the southeastern markets. Due to a recent retirement, a regional SVP position had opened up. Although Jameson had not had Libby top of mind for the position, recent research, inspired by the PR crisis, into eligible female candidates brought her name to the top. He planned to name her to the position and issue a full press release regarding the promotion.

When Libby received the call from Betty, she automatically thought she was going to be laid off. She knew the company was in the midst of restructuring, and the retirement of John Franklin, her regional SVP, led Libby to the conclusion that the new SVP would want his own hand-selected team. It took Betty three tries to explain that the meeting was not about Libby's dismissal but rather to discuss future opportunities. Jameson had requested that Libby prepare a strategic regional thirty-sixty-ninety-day sales plan for the meeting; he also requested that she look at the current staffing of the regional sales teams and come up with suggestions for consolidation while keeping in mind "the current PR climate." Furthermore, the reissued RFP requesting more detailed D&I data came from this region. Betty sent over a list of all direct sales positions with their last two quarterly evaluations.

You may want to learn a little more about Libby. She is forty-six years old, divorced, and has no children. Of northern European descent, Libby is a graduate of the University of Pennsylvania. She has devoted the last fifteen years of her life to the company, and readily admits that her dedication to her work may have been a contributing factor in her failed twenty-year marriage. She took her position as a part-time life insurance representative when her husband lost his job. While she and her husband had planned that she would only work temporarily, until their finances improved, Libby found that she liked the work and she was really good at it as well. She won Sales Rep of the Year for five years straight (a company record) before she was promoted to sales manager.

Life at All Vector was not easy for Libby. She was often the only woman at management events, and at corporate social events she was often asked what area her husband managed. Libby did not want to be seen as a whiner so she took it all in stride and did her best to fit in with the team. Before the merger, she was being recruited by Strong Choice for a VP sales role. She was impressed with their diverse culture and saw a genuine opportunity to move her career forward. Libby was in her second interview when news broke that the two companies were in merger discussions.

Libby knew she had a lot of work to do to prepare for her upcoming meeting with Jameson. This could be a big break for her. Before she had a chance to look at the sales team files, one of her recent recruits, Mai, knocked on her door. This was Mai's first position after graduating from UCLA—she had been recruited as part of the campus program. A first-generation American, Mai was of Vietnamese descent. Libby wanted to tap the Chinese market for life insurance, and she assigned that demographic to Mai. Although Libby knew Mai was of Vietnamese origin, she thought Mai would be better received than the other campus recruit, Chandler, a Southern white guy. Mai had high hopes for her first job, but was finding it difficult to fit in with the rest of the team. She wanted a chance to make a big splash. Mai thought that the Chinese market would be limiting to her career prospects. Also, she was not sure whether Libby knew she was not Chinese and she did not know how to broach the subject. She did not speak Chinese at all and was unfamiliar with Chinese American culture. After three months at the company, Mai was not meeting her sales plan and wanted Libby to reassign her to another market.

We will follow Jameson, Libby, and Mai throughout the book. Their stories will reflect some common struggles at the executive, middle management, and individual contributor levels when it comes to diversity and inclusion. Although their challenges may be different, they will strive for the same goal of creating an inclusive culture.

Owner v. Renter

All three will face what we call the *owner-versus-renter dilemma.* At this point in time they are squarely in the renter's box. So what do we mean by the owner-versus-renter dilemma? It is actually a mind-set every one of us takes when it comes to areas of responsibility. Before we explain the term's use at the corporate level, let's look at it from a common perspective. At some point in our lives, many of us have rented a place to live or a car. Think about how you treated the rental. In the case of the apartment, did you paint it? Did you take on any upkeep? When a faucet start leaking did you get right on it and fix it, or did you put it on a mental list to let the landlord know at some point? If it was a car you rented, did you ride it a little harder, not worry about the oil, put in the cheaper gas, or park it in areas where it might be exposed to damage?

Now let's think about a time you owned the place you lived in. If the faucet started leaking, did you fix it right away? Did you keep up on the painting? Did you make sure to change the central air filters on a regular basis? If you owned your car, did you tend to put in better gas, check the oil, and park it in a spot where it was less likely to get dinged? It is human nature for us to treat things differently if we own them. The same goes for workplace practices. If we feel as though safety is someone else's concern—maybe someone with the word "safety" in her title—then we might not pay too much attention to creating a safe environment. Although we may not say it, subconsciously we are relegating those tasks to someone else. What would the culture of a manufacturer be if workers thought safety was only the duty of those who had "safety" in their titles? It would be a very unhealthy environment. Safety is a workplace practice that is instilled at every level at manufacturers, from the CEO to the plant floor workers. Of course, you would expect chemical plants to put a lot of emphasis on safety, and companies such as DuPont own safety everywhere. As you walk through DuPont's buildings you will find employees holding onto handrails as they ascend or descend staircases. They pay particular attention to safety at the beginning of each meeting, regardless of whether it is in the boardroom or the lab. They own safety.

Other companies, such as those in the banking industry, have instilled a sense of ownership when it comes to data security. As we work with global banks, we have come to notice that every employee understands and owns data security as something that is part of their responsibility regardless of their title or position. So how does this relate to diversity and inclusion?

Let's look first at Jameson. Do you think he owns D&I, or is he just a renter? An owner would take on development and direction of inclusion as part of his job responsibilities. Executives can easily wave off D&I as the sole responsibility of the D&I team, or as part of HR's sphere of influence. As with the safety and data security examples above, only a handful of people in any organization have titles that relate specifically to inclusion. There is no way they can lead a workforce of tens of thousands unless the executive team takes on inclusion as one of its core responsibilities. However, the executive team cannot shoulder that responsibility alone. As we follow Libby's path, continually ask yourself if she is owning or just renting inclusion. Organizations need management from line to middle to senior level to commit themselves to owning D&I as one of their core functions.

Surely, we cannot expect an individual contributor like Mai to take on ownership of diversity and inclusion, right? Wrong. D&I is not an initiative that management alone needs to foster. Management admittedly shoulders more responsibility: they set the policies, procedures, and practices for the organization. The company culture typically reflects the values expressed by management. That does not, however, get individual contributors off the hook. Individual contributors make up the bulk of a company's staff, and they are also the majority of client-facing employees. How they behave and interact has a huge influence on the culture of inclusion, and employee resource groups (ERGs) rely on individual contributors to fill the majority of their membership. It is safe to say that neither Jameson, Libby, nor Mai is fully owning diversity and inclusion as a core responsibility of his or her own at the moment. As their stories unfold in each chapter, you may find this dynamic shifting.

A Look Ahead

Before we go further, we should give you a high-level map of the path you are about to embark on. You have just been introduced to our three main characters. In chapter 1, on self-awareness, their challenge will be a hurdle of awareness for themselves, but they must also become acutely aware of their unique surroundings. In chapter 2, our characters will need to think about their newfound awareness from a different angle by becoming a little less automatic and a little more reflective in their decision making. All of this new knowledge would be for naught if they failed to take action: in chapter 3, they will be implementing an action plan that will help them realize their workplace goals by owning inclusion as a core function.

As we tell the stories of Jameson, Libby, and Mai and apply SET, we will be speaking about inclusion concepts. We highly recommend you leverage *The Inclusion Dividend* to take a deeper dive on any of the concepts that pique your interest. The book was specifically written in a nonlinear fashion, so you can hop from one chapter to the next without losing much context.

Some of the topics and dynamics that show up consistently in the stories are insider–outsider dynamics, unconscious bias, and intent versus impact. *The Inclusion Dividend* devotes a full chapter to both unconscious bias and insider–outsider dynamics, as well as considerable space to the concept of intent versus impact. At the end of each of those chapters are summary learning points and discussion guides to further draw out the reading. *SET for Inclusion* is meant to provide you with a method for applying those concepts in an easy and memorable fashion to almost any decision. Although we will be speaking to decisions that directly impact internal employees and external clients, SET can be applied to almost any decision. Some insurance companies are leveraging this approach when it comes to setting risk for policies, while others are applying it to corporate acquisitions. We have even heard from a couple of attendees who used SET in their personal lives with family and friends. Although we will be steering you toward making inclusive decisions that involve people in your workplace, feel free to keep your mind open to other applications as well.

Need for Development Arises

Libby's upcoming meeting with Jameson was about to start the two on their path to leveraging SET. Their two-hour meeting ended up being forty-five minutes due to a late-running investor meeting Jameson was leading. Libby found her meeting with Jameson to be rather perfunctory, as if they were both just going through the motions and a decision had already been made. Unknown to Libby, Jameson had planned to promote her to SVP even before they talked. One point that did spark up conversation was the reissued RFP that was questioning VeStrong's commitment to diversity. Libby noted that one of the questions asked specifically to what extent VeStrong had developed leaders on mitigating unconscious bias. She had done her homework, and related to Jameson not only the gist of the question but also that she discovered VeStrong did not have any programs in place that touched upon this subject. Libby had taken the liberty of reaching out to contacts in other companies to get recommendations for consulting firms that specialized in this area. She told Jameson that they could get a pilot going within thirty days, before the RFP was due. Jameson agreed that it would look good for them to pilot it at a cross section of levels, from individual contributors to his executive team.

The Dagoba Group was chosen to develop Jameson's

executive team and the SVPs, including Libby, while also doing a separate pilot workshop for Libby's sales team. The consulting team researched VeStrong's current situation via interviews, sponsor discussions, and data review. We established learning objectives and concluded that an inclusive leadership workshop that combined concepts of unconscious bias and insider–outsider dynamics was the most appropriate fit.

It is probably about time we got Jameson, Libby, and Mai started on their learning journey. At the end of each chapter, we have provided some key takeaways for future reference. Feel free to write, either on a blank sheet of paper or in the pages of your copy of the book, anything these stories inspire in you.

As always, we love hearing your stories. Please write us at Info@TheDagobaGroup.com about how you have applied the concepts in this book to your workplace or personal life. Whether you had successes or challenges, we want to hear them. We grow and learn by reading your stories, as we hope you will grow and learn with this book.

Key Takeaways

- ✓ Diversity and inclusion development needs to provide practical implementation.
- ✓ Awareness is necessary, but not sufficient.
- ✓ Application of learning concepts are only successful if they are memorable.
- ✓ Everyone in the organization should own the responsibility of creating an inclusive environment.

1

Self-Awareness

Common sense is the collection of prejudices
acquired by age eighteen.
—Albert Einstein

Think of any behavioral change you have ever made. Perhaps you started an exercise program. Maybe you made an effort to reduce the amount of time you spent watching TV. Or possibly you tried a new, healthier diet. Self-awareness is always the starting point for any change effort, be it personal, professional, or organizational. When it comes to inclusive leadership, self-awareness is particularly critical. However, self-awareness is often impeded by a well-intentioned individual's resistance to the notion that she is not an inclusive leader. In our decades of working with leaders across the globe, we have concluded that the vast majority of leaders are well intentioned when it comes to being inclusive and to working effectively with an increasingly diverse workforce and marketplace. However, we have talked to enough staff and seen enough data to know that that a leader's intent doesn't always align with the experience of those who work for the company—that is, good intentions don't necessarily translate to real impact in the workplace. The SET model is all about aligning intent and impact. Self-awareness is the first step.

In *The Inclusion Dividend* we wrote in detail about two inclusion concepts (unconscious bias and insider–outsider dynamics) that we believe can create misalignment between a leader's inclusive intent and the resulting exclusive impact on a diverse group of staff and clients. Both concepts are predictable human dynamics that often interfere with inclusive treatment. Unconscious bias is about how our acquired preconceptions can interfere with our inclusive intent by reinforcing stereotypes and keeping us in our comfort zone, thus reinforcing the status quo. Insider–outsider dynamics create an un-level playing field by making it easier for some groups to succeed than others. Both dynamics operate in the background of our decision making, often without us knowing they are shaping our behavior. Thus, both dynamics become implicit and are seen mostly by the individuals and groups being negatively impacted. In this way, these dynamics present a dilemma when it comes to creating self-awareness.

Starting Point for Awareness

How does one become aware of something that is unconscious or implicit? The starting point for self-awareness, when it comes to being an inclusive leader, requires a leap of faith. We all need to accept that our decisions, regardless of our conscious beliefs, may be influenced by unconscious bias or insider–outsider dynamics. If you are a human being, you are going to carry unconscious biases and be affected by insider–outsider dynamics. Jameson and Mai, whom we met in the introduction, embody this challenge. Jameson has been around awhile, is well-intentioned, and believes himself to be "blind" to a person's visible differences. In fact, he would likely be quite offended by the notion that there is anything but a level playing field at VeStrong, or previously at All Vector, for that matter. Leaders sometimes see an admission that their organization is not a true meritocracy as a negative judgment against themselves, drawing doubt about their achievements. On the contrary, a true meritocracy is a pursuit and not an actual destination. Admitting you do not have a true meritocracy simply allows the organization to continue the pursuit.

Jameson does not see himself as a member of any sort of demographic group, particularly when it comes to gender, race, age, or most other important aspects of difference. Mai, on the other hand, has a clear sense of herself as a member of her ethnic and gender group. As hard as it is for Jameson to "see" his own ethnic group as a differentiator, it is just as hard for Mai to not understand herself as both an individual and a woman of Vietnamese descent. Self-awareness is most challenging when we are trying to understand our insider groups. It would be difficult for Jameson to accept the likelihood, or even the possibility, that some kind of non-inclusive behavior was at play at VeStrong.

A real-life example of this internal challenge could be seen in orchestras that, though they expressed the good intent to hire the best musicians, were mostly hiring men.

In 1970, the top five U.S. orchestras were made up of more than 95 percent men. Blind auditions were instituted so the judges could not determine the gender of the musician, which increased the likelihood of women being called back for a second audition by 50 percent. *The Voice,* a popular TV show, pivots on this bias, as judges are not allowed to see the performer until they have decided to choose him or her, so race, ethnicity, and other dimensions of difference are not apparent during the selection process. Just because you want the best does not mean you are choosing the best.

We firmly believe, though, that engaging from our insider group memberships needs to be the starting point for increasing self-awareness. When we first began doing diversity work, this was certainly not an accepted starting point. Many participants in traditional diversity workshops had a perception that the training course was designed to prove to them that they were bad people. This method didn't create productive conversations, as most of us perceive ourselves as good people, and the vast majority are well intentioned. The other starting point for many (often for outsiders) was that the training didn't apply to them—that they were already behaving in an inclusive way simply because they were members of an outsider group. Part of the problem is that we often don't see that we have multiple insider and outsider groups. Jameson is a white man, while Mai is a woman of color. On both race and gender, their starting points for self-awareness are very different. However, perhaps on sexual orientation they are both in the insider heterosexual group, and thus their starting point for self-awareness is similar for that aspect. On the issue of age, Jameson may be experiencing himself as transitioning from the insider group to the outsider group, and his self-awareness will likely begin to shift. Mai might be quite unaware (as she is likely in the insider group on generational difference) of the impact of her age. The challenge of self-awareness does not lie with Jameson alone.

Libby sits in an interesting position. As a white woman in her forties who was raised fully in Eurocentric American culture, she can relate to Mai as a woman, but when it comes to age, race, and culture, she is likely to be as unaware of the dynamics as Jameson is with regard to gender. You can see that there are substantial challenges to increasing self-awareness. Libby sits in the middle, structurally. She is a middle manager, and thus is much closer to the action and much closer to the most diverse part of the organization. In the majority of organizations, the transition from high diversity to a less-diverse profile is the inflection point from middle to senior management. Jameson looks at middle management as the source of the problem on many issues. Mai does the same, as her day-to-day experiences and interactions are largely shaped by middle management. Libby carries much of the blame in either direction.

So each of our characters enters the pilot workshop with different starting points. What binds them, though, is the business case for inclusion. They have a shared interest in the success of the business. This interest is the starting point for our pilot workshop; it is the compelling reason they are in the room and the clear goal that they all share. There is a generic business case to be made: being inclusive is a good thing, as it engages more people, provides more perspectives, and helps the business identify opportunities more quickly and fully. However, each of our three characters needs to make a personal connection to the business case; the business case needs to be real for each one. Each has to identify his or her own unique inclusion dividend.

Identifying Their Inclusion Dividend

For Mai, the business case is connected directly to developing more exposure internally and externally so her skill sets can be seen beyond her group memberships. She's realized that if she is pigeonholed into working only with the Asian market, her earnings potential and career opportunities may be limited. This narrow assignment is exacerbated when the Asian market is seen in a monolithic way, when Mai knows how much diversity exists across Asian cultures. For sure, Mai's style and approach might resonate in some parts of this vast and growing market, but her style and approach are likely much more broadly applicable.

For Jameson, the immediate inclusion dividend is to get in front of potentially bad publicity and better position the company as an attractive financial partner in the marketplace. Jameson, though, could also connect to a more substantial and long-lasting inclusion dividend. If the leadership in his business continues to be a non-diverse group, over time it is likely that the business will grow more slowly and innovate less. This will be a huge lost opportunity in an industry where the customer base is rapidly becoming more diverse.

Libby has perhaps the most granular and important business case. Like many middle managers, she sits just above the slice of the organization with the highest degree of diversity. Her ability to harness and develop this diverse talent will quite directly impact her career success and earnings. Research increasingly demonstrates that diverse teams, when led in an inclusive manner, outperform non-diverse teams. If Libby steps up to this challenge, learning how to lead inclusively, both she and the organization will be handsomely rewarded.

Levels of Systems

We are starting our self-awareness focus at the biggest "level of system"—the market. We believe if we can do this successfully, then the path to individual-level awareness and inclusive leadership behavior is easier. VeStrong is a for-profit enterprise, and any significant strategy or change initiative must be fully connected to enhancing shareholder value. A full exploration of the business case—or self-awareness at the market level of system—also connects our characters to their good intent. Why would any business leader not want to act and lead inclusively? The challenge and opportunity to translate this inclusive intention into an inclusive impact will become clear.

With Jameson, Libby, and Mai connected to their own potential inclusion dividends, they are ready to "get granular" and engage self-awareness at the individual level. To do this they will have to understand how unconscious bias and insider–outsider dynamics are affecting their perspectives and behaviors. This means going from the biggest level of system—the marketplace—to the individual level.

Self-Awareness at the Individual Level

Unconscious bias creates a dilemma for every individual when it comes to self-awareness: How can I become aware of something that is unconscious? This is a good question, and it speaks to the iterative nature of increasing self-awareness in the area of human interaction. There is always more to learn, differences are limitless, the world is getting smaller, business is increasingly global, and, in short, we will never be done learning about other people and how to interact with them effectively. The work of Mahzarin Banaji and Anthony Greenwald in creating the Harvard Implicit Association Test has helped in the pursuit of increased self-awareness. These online tests allow users to examine their level of unconscious bias on nearly three dozen aspects of diversity. Millions of people have taken the test, creating a vast research database. The experience of many test takers parallels the dilemma in increasing self-awareness about our own unconscious biases, in that the user estimates his own level of bias before taking the test and then often finds that his biases are stronger than he predicted. The research behind this test, and the related research just in the past fifteen years, provides a very clear picture that unconscious bias is typical, pervasive, and impactful. Thus, the first step in self-awareness is to take a leap of faith and accept that if you are human you likely carry many unconscious biases. The leadership opportunity involves finding ways to control for those biases in your decision making. Leaders make many decisions on any given day, and a lot of these decisions impact people. It is clear that up to this point our colleague Jameson is not ready to take this leap. He embodies the state of the insider group: well-intended ignorance.

To raise self-awareness at the individual level it is important to think about these daily, moment-to-moment decisions that involve and impact people. Almost everything a leader does involves people in some way. Many of these decisions are ones that require conscious thought, clear focus, and considerable time, such as who to hire, who to fire, and who to promote. Most leaders know these are critical decisions and they want the decisions to be as fair and objective as possible. Often, however, it is the daily, small, rapport-building behaviors that ultimately have a strong influence on those larger decisions. In this way, the big decisions can seem to be fair, objective, and performance-based, while the daily experiences that influence performance and reflect unconscious bias are missed.

Think about the little decisions we make, the ones we are often not aware of. We make decisions about who to say hello to when we walk into the office in the morning, decisions about who to chat with informally, decisions about who to engage over coffee or lunch, decisions about who to include in important meetings, whose e-mail to return first, even whose desk to stop at for a quick check-in as we return from a meeting. These are just a handful of the decisions we make every day that involve people and have the potential to reflect unconscious bias. All of our typical behavior is only intensified when we are under pressure, because when we are under pressure we tend to stay in our comfort zone and go with what we know. Thus, unconscious bias is self-reinforcing.

As Jameson thinks about these little decisions some light-bulbs begin to go on. He is seeing clearly that his day-to-day life is shaped by people who are mostly like him; he has been connecting most closely with the people who have much in common with him. "Perhaps it is not a coincidence that the senior team is so non-diverse," he thinks. On the other hand, the men he knows the best have been putting a lot of effort into both their work and their visibility. Those are job skills that should be rewarded. He glances at Libby and wonders why she hasn't gone out of her way to connect with him. After all, being a go-getter is a characteristic important to success in his business. Even a high performer like Libby doesn't get on his radar screen in a significant way. He can't recall her reaching out to him for any sort of special project or visible opportunity. She doesn't come to mind first because he doesn't have a good sense of who she is. Mai, many levels below Jameson and in the horizontal slice of the organization that is the most diverse, is not known to Jameson at all. Jameson does acknowledge, though, that the newer recruited staff is more and more diverse.

Libby is thinking about these issues from both sides. As a woman she sees clearly how the "little things" accumulate to the advantage of her male peers. Her response to that is to put her head down and work that much harder. She can't be a man, but she can try to outwork them. She is proud of her approach and her success, but it has taken a toll. She is also wondering about the downside of her approach; she has probably undermined herself at times. The workshop prereading included the April 2014 *Forbes* article, "Act Now to Shrink the Confidence Gap," which noted a Hewlett Packard study that found that men will reach for a position/assignment when they believe they meet 60 percent of the qualifications, whereas women wait until they believe they meet 100 percent of the qualifications. Indeed, Libby can think of some times when she should've been more aggressive in going after opportunities. The other thing on Libby's mind is her team. The facilitator said something about how "we are all in it together" when it comes to unconscious bias...that everyone is biased. Libby gets that at a high level but hasn't really considered it more granularly. "How are my biases affecting my diverse team?" she wonders. Libby's team is quite diverse, but her highest performers are white.

Mai finds the discussion of unconscious bias quite interesting. She is noticing the engagement of many of her colleagues and is cautiously optimistic that the leaders in the other workshop are gleaning some important insights. The conversation about the small behaviors that reflect unconscious bias resonates for her. She has experienced and observed these little behaviors since she started her career. At first she thought it was just rudeness, cultural difference, or personality differences. Now she sees the larger pattern because, taken together, the behaviors make it harder for her to be treated as a full member of the team. Sometimes she has to overdo it just to get attention, and that is uncomfortable. Lately she has been withdrawing from team conversations, tuning out, and not even trying to make contributions.

As she sits in the workshop Mai realizes she has a lot to add, but she holds back. She doesn't want to say much, as it is uncomfortable to be the focus of a D&I conversation given that she is a member of several of the groups that the senior leaders are trying to understand. She recalls an African American colleague, Janet, who spoke more openly about some of these challenges, and she noticed that Janet's points were not well received and that she was seen as oversensitive. Mai does not want to be the "poster child" of diversity but she doesn't want to be invisible either, so she is beginning to think about where she might have unconscious biases. One of her peers is a gay man. She likes Richard a lot and they sometimes have lunch together. She is very careful, though, not to ask him to join her for client meetings as she thinks the clients may not be as comfortable with Richard as she is. "I wonder if this is my unconscious bias?" she thinks.

A critical step in increasing self-awareness is to assume that unconscious bias influences our day-to-day decisions; it is only once we acknowledge unconscious biases that we can take steps to control for that bias. To develop our self-awareness we have to focus our efforts on small decisions and behaviors, and acknowledge how unconscious bias can impact them. What would Jameson see if he looked at his day-to-day behavior? Libby might have some insight. She is a top-performing sales manager, so it is surprising that Jameson didn't know her better. One wonders about the extent of their interaction. Perhaps Jameson is interacting primarily with long-standing employees who are most like him. How well did he know Libby, how she thinks, and what makes her successful? If he knew her better perhaps she wouldn't have been interviewing with Strong Choice at the time of the merger. Libby wasn't considered for the SVP role until the company was in crisis mode over diversity. Inclusion that is sustainable starts at the beginning of an employee's life with the company and involves literally hundreds or thousands of interactions over time, the kinds of interactions that grease the wheels of a relationship, build rapport and trust, and ultimately open up opportunities for employees at all levels to be visible and grow.

To increase our self-awareness we need to begin to understand these three interconnected factors: 1) our experiences, 2) what we have learned (including stereotypes), and 3) our comfort zone.

Generally, we build relationships most easily with people who are like us, and this can create a reinforcing cycle. When people we are comfortable with get opportunities, we often see them succeed, and this creates a self-fulfilling prophecy. Thus, there is a positive reinforcing cycle as our comfort zone is fortified and our experiences remain largely the same. Stereotypes come from multiple sources and include the information and associations we have learned directly and indirectly. This chapter started with a quote from Albert Einstein: "Common sense is the collection of prejudices acquired by age eighteen." He was not that far off. In a July 2014 *Pacific Standard* article, "How Stereotypes Take Place," the authors highlight a University of Aberdeen study that speaks to how easily and early our minds process information into categories, creating "a progressively simplified, highly structured, and easily learnable system of stereotypes." This information sits in our unconscious brain and affects our judgments and behavior.

Think about Jameson's upbringing and how early his preconceptions were set. The same might be true for Libby. Mai certainly carries her own set of stereotypes but she also likely has substantial experience confronting stereotypes directly, as she's helped her immigrant parents navigate a new culture and worked to show herself in ways that will enhance her career. Ironically, many of the stereotypes we hold would be rejected by our conscious mind, however, the majority of our judgments and decisions rely on our unconscious mind. Therein lies the self-awareness challenge for the individual with inclusive intentions. Our experiences are often molded by our stereotypes and our comfort zone. Later we will talk about how to increase self-awareness; one way to do this is to change our experiences.

We have been talking primarily about awareness at the individual level. For a leader who wishes to lead inclusive teams, create an inclusive climate, and lead an inclusive business—in other words, achieve inclusion dividends—awareness starts at the individual level but extends to the team and organizational levels as well. In the SET framework, awareness must be increased at all levels if inclusion initiatives are to be sustainable.

Self-Awareness at the Group and Team Levels

Little work gets done individually in most organizations. Increasingly, we work in teams, and often those teams are virtual. An important self-awareness challenge is to understand how insider–outsider dynamics show up on teams. Insider–outsider dynamics permeate all teams, affecting interactions, relationships, and, ultimately, opportunities. Unconscious bias, in fact, shows up most powerfully when it works to the advantage of insider groups and to the disadvantage of outsider groups. Understanding insider–outsider dynamics requires being able to notice patterns of experience that are based on group identity. These patterns are about the experiences that team members have that are connected to their various insider and outsider groups and about which group's norms are favored in various settings.

Between Jameson, Libby, and Mai there are a number of group identities and thus several insider–outsider dynamics at play. Gender is an obvious one, as is race. Age is likely a factor, and culture is potentially at play as well. Level of hierarchy is itself an insider–outsider group (management–nonmanagement). Hierarchy exacerbates the other insider and outsider groups because there is probably less diversity near the top of the organization and more near the bottom. Mai, who has a number of outsider group memberships, will likely have the most awareness of the patterns related to being in the insider or outsider group. She is likely one of very few women of color on the team, possibly the only Asian American. While raised in the United States, she is likely heavily influenced by her parents' culture, and thus culture may have an impact on her experience as well. She will likely find it hard to build close, easy relationships with her colleagues, who may have a perception of her related to her gender and ethnicity. Libby's classing of Mai with other Asian groups that are different from her own is likely a pattern she has experienced before.

Similarly, Libby's struggle to be visible is likely an ongoing challenge she has faced in a male-dominated sales management culture. She is likely to have a good sense of the patterns women faced at All Vector, and these patterns probably impacted her decision to interview with another company. Jameson will likely have little awareness of any patterns related to gender, race, culture, or position because he is in the insider group on all of those aspects of diversity. Jameson's lack of awareness is not a reflection of his intent, it is merely a by-product of insider–outsider dynamics. This will be one of Jameson's biggest blind spots, and becoming aware of these dynamics is central to his ability to be an inclusive leader.

These blindspot challenges became increasingly apparent in the workshop. The group brainstormed all of the insider and outsider groups that have an impact in the organization. The one that people seemed to have the most energy for was the legacy organizations—whether employees had worked for All Vector or Strong Choice. This is quite a live issue given the merger. Mai was struck by how many of the traditional diversity issues were not being put on the list. These are the issues that most impact Mai: gender, race, and ethnicity. The group seemed to want to talk mostly about the issues where they were in the outsider group, those that weren't "loaded" and hard to talk about. While Mai found the conversation interesting, and actually noticed that she had a few insider groups she hadn't thought about, she wondered whether this workshop was going to be helpful at all. "Maybe this is going to be another safe conversation that won't go anywhere," she thought. Mai could've easily added several more groups to the list but she held back. She smiled when Richard finally wrote up "straight" as an insider group and "gay" as outsider.

Libby was thinking along the same lines as Mai, but she decided to try something. She remembered a piece of feedback from a member of her staff who was located in a regional office. She added "headquarters" as an insider group and "regions" as outsider. The facilitator noticed that she had written up one of her insider groups and commented that insiders often aren't aware of their group. John, a white male colleague, looked at Libby and then wrote "men" and "women." The conversation that followed was very interesting. Many of the participants were struck by how many insider and outsider groups had been brainstormed so quickly. Jameson looked sobered. He realized that he was an insider on almost every issue, except for age. Age was the only issue that he had contributed.

At the group and team level there are some key indicators for awareness. These show up as the "patterns of experience" we have been talking about. One key indicator has to do with relationships on the team. This plays out via patterns of interaction on teams. Beyond an individual's own level of skill, very little gets done in most companies without effective interaction. Having membership in key insider groups often provides a level of ease in creating a network of relationships, and affinity has a real impact here. Another is the norms that the team uses to get its work done. These norms are important to understand because they represent the "culture" of the team. They will tend to reflect the norms of insider groups. For example, in most U.S.-based companies, these norms will reflect an extraverted style, with lots of brainstorming, the loudest voice getting the attention, and, structurally, a collaborative way of doing work. A third key indicator is the opportunities to demonstrate leadership on the team. This is about power and who finds it easiest to exercise power and influence. Visible leadership on the team is often the key factor in being seen as having potential or being viewed as promotable. Opportunities to lead aren't just cosmetic; they provide real experience, offering chances to learn, experiment, fail, and get feedback—the things that all leaders have to learn.

To increase your self-awareness at the group and team level, you must be able to see patterns of experience around each of these key indicators. It is important not to individualize everything. Libby is an extremely successful sales manager, yet she is not visible with a key leader like Jameson—is that just Libby's problem? Is there something she should've been doing differently to manage her career? She probably could have done some things differently or could have "leaned in" just a bit more, as popular author and executive Sheryl Sandberg would advise. However, if Libby's experience is similar to what other women in the company have experienced, then this is a pattern and there is something more at play than Libby's actions. The key questions to ask to raise your awareness at the group and team level are about the patterns that exist on your team that seem to be related more to team members' insider and outsider groups than to their individual qualities. This requires transcending individuality and looking at patterns.

Who speaks more, women or men? How often do minorities on the team speak first? Do team members in the regional offices participate less on team calls than those located at headquarters? What is the typical demographic profile of the team members who seem to do the most socializing or informal interacting? Libby needs to look at patterns as well. She manages sales teams. What kind of environment does she create on her teams? How easy is it for Mai, especially if she is the only Asian woman, to participate and have a voice in team meetings? Libby needs to notice patterns of participation and not assume that they only reflect the skill or ability of individuals on the team. Perhaps the U.S.-born white men are the ones who seem to do the most initiating. Does this mean they are more intelligent or competent? As noted earlier in the *Forbes* article, men are much more likely to raise their hand for an assignment earlier than women. Many Asians will be less apt to talk about their accomplishments openly. Laura Liswood speaks to this cultural norm in her book *The Loudest Duck*; in Asia the loudest duck gets shot (negative association with extraverts), while in the U.S. the squeaky wheel gets mended first (positive association with extraverts). Introverts are less likely to engage in large group meetings, particularly when the pace is fast. These are all patterns of participation based more upon group identities than individual capability. As a leader, to inclusively engage a diverse team you will first need to be able to see these patterns.

Self-Awareness at the Organizational Level

Ultimately, as a leader you must engage the paradox of managing everyone as individuals while simultaneously being fully aware of the impact of their group memberships. Doing that well requires understanding how each individual's insider and outsider groups impact her ability to be successful and make her full contribution. You also have to understand the key organizational levers that enable success and progression. This involves increasing your awareness about how unconscious bias and insider–outsider dynamics impact all of the talent-related processes in your organization. These include everything from résumé screening, the interview and selection process for candidates, onboarding, talent assessment, development and review, and the promotion process.

Jameson was taken aback by the insider–outsider conversation. He is now seriously wondering if the new organization is preparing a more diverse future leadership pipeline—or if it is just re-creating the past. In the discussions over the last few weeks about the absence of women in leadership, many of his peers talked about the women middle managers as not having "what it takes," lacking the gravitas or presence to be strong leaders. "Maybe the way we assess and develop leaders isn't very inclusive," he thinks. If Libby could read Jameson's mind she would be nodding vigorously. She has often felt that the system was stacked against her, and that she had to try to be somebody she was not if she wanted to get ahead.

Unintentional bias that favors insider groups over outsider groups can be subtly embedded in these systems and processes. For example, the schools that are favored for recruiting can significantly impact the kind of candidates selected. When interview panels and talent review panels are non-diverse, their results will tend reflect that sameness. Libby recalls her interview at All Vector. She was the only woman, with the exception of the HR rep, whom she saw in the entire interview process. At the time, she put that aside and focused on making the best possible impression, however she now wonders how many women actually make it through that process. The competencies that employees are being assessed against sometimes reflect an out of date or unnecessarily narrow definition of success. To paraphrase another Einstein quote, "If you judge a fish by its ability to climb a tree, it will live its whole corporate life believing that it will never succeed." Often, corporations discover that a position's tree-climbing qualification had absolutely nothing valid to do with performing in the role, and more to do with what a leader at some point in the company's history thought was a needed "fit" for that position.

Perhaps Mai's more low-key style wasn't viewed as representing high potential. Perhaps Libby's lack of relationships with senior leaders meant that her name didn't come up often in talent review meetings, which were attended by a non-diverse group of senior leaders.

Why is it important to be aware at the organizational level? If unintended bias isn't addressed, it will lead to the perpetuation of sameness in the organization. There will be many well-intentioned leaders who simply won't realize the factors at play that create a non-diverse demographic profile high up in the organization. These leaders may see the business case but not know what to do, or they may try to solve the wrong problem.

Becoming more aware at the organizational level requires three activities: 1) measuring the impact on diversity of the company's organizational talent processes, 2) taking a good look at all talent-related processes and asking where bias might be embedded in the process itself, and 3) understanding which behaviors are being rewarded and reinforced and which aren't.

Continuing the Story: Increasing Self-Awareness at All Levels

Before the workshop, Jameson was at dinner and thinking about Libby's promotion and the associated PR campaign. He mentioned his plans casually to his wife and children.

His daughter was visiting for the week, as she was taking a vacation from her job as an investment banker. His son was between terms at graduate school. Jameson's wife mentioned that she thought it might seem a bit odd to make such fanfare over Libby's promotion: "Why are you making such a big deal out of this? I thought you promoted people based on performance, not gender." His daughter pointed out that it seemed hypocritical, especially since he promoted so few women. She said, "The last thing I would want is to be made unusually visible—it would just make people think I was promoted because I am a woman. Is that why you promoted her?" His daughter also asked him why so few women had been promoted. She'd noticed this pattern in her company but hoped it was changing. His son gave him an "I think they are right" smile.

At his desk the next morning, Jameson pondered the dinner conversation and decided he needed to get his head around this situation. He started to think about Libby and why she was the only female candidate for a senior-level position. He thought about his key relationships in the company. Later, in the workshop, he wrote these relationships down. All were white men, and most were in his age group. Every one of his close connections was from All Vector. He thought about his network outside of the company. They were all men. This quick audit of his key professional relationships made him cringe a little bit. He tried to reason away the lack of diversity in his relationships by ascribing it to the nature of the industry. But he also knew that the demographics in the industry were beginning to change. More of his peers at other companies were women. This was also true with more and more clients. And it didn't stop with women. Growth markets were more frequently culturally and ethnically diverse. So far it hadn't affected the business too much, but he figured that would change. In fact, he was increasingly thinking about the operations in the Asia–Pacific region. Growth was fast and operations were increasingly moving to both East and South Asia. He'd noticed at recruiting events and all-division meetings the increase in gender, ethnic, and cultural differences; he realized he didn't know much about these employees and that he interacted with them rarely.

In his mind, though, he kept coming back to meritocracy. He and his peers thoroughly vetted the key promotions into management. They made those choices based on performance and a balance of other factors that they know fit the profile of a high achiever in the industry. Also, these executives were, while a bit old-fashioned, a good group of people and all well intentioned as far as Jameson could tell. He was clear about his management team's intent but was increasingly aware that the impact of their actions was not aligned with the intent. He decided he had to begin to take ownership of this issue. It was time to act.

The situation at VeStrong is disturbingly common. D&I gets considered at the back end, after it has become a considerable problem, often when others have raised concerns. Increasing self-awareness helps to force a consideration of D&I sooner.

Jameson is trying to fix the problem on the back end. He realizes that other stakeholders are looking at what they can see—the statistics of diverse representation. They are unable to see the day-to-day dynamics that are creating those results. If Jameson doesn't increase his self-awareness about those daily dynamics then he won't be able to do anything that is sustainable and effective. Libby and Mai also need to put their self-awareness to work. Mai must be careful not to feed a self-fulfilling prophecy by feeling completely disempowered. She needs to keep her eyes open and look for places to use her perspective to help both her career and the organization. Libby has perhaps the biggest day-to-day challenge. Like Mai, she has to empower herself. Like Jameson, she has to create more awareness of the day-to-day dynamics on the team that reports to her now and the teams that will work for her after her promotion.

Key Takeaways

- ✓ Self-awareness is more powerful when done on four levels of systems: individual, group/team, organizational, and marketplace.
- ✓ The first step to self-awareness is to measure your exposure to difference.
- ✓ Realize that unconscious bias is human and that to be leaders we need to manage these biases.
- ✓ Self-awareness is necessary but not sufficient for enacting change.
- ✓ Focusing only on individual behavior will not create sustainable change. Systemic barriers need to be broken down.

2

Engage System 2

Make it a point to expose yourself to difference every day. This is the golden rule for acquiring the habit of engaging System 2.

—*The Dagoba Group*

In the previous chapter, our three colleagues achieved a heightened sense of awareness. Often, this is where organizations start and end when it comes to D&I development. Those "aha" moments are necessary, but they are far from sufficient. This is analogous to your mechanic enlightening you on why your brakes are squeaking. If it stops there, all you have is a story to tell, but no way to avoid the same issues down the road. The whole goal of development should be to improve the outcome. At The Dagoba Group, we completely understand that, whether you are in the C-suite or on the front line, you have more competing priorities than you can count. When development opportunities take you away from your desk for any amount of time, you need an outcome that goes beyond making you aware of the problem. If you are investing your personal time and organizational resources, you need to realize a measureable return.

Historically, there has been powerful awareness work done in the area of diversity and inclusion. Because our group identities so often shape our experiences invisibly, perceptions can sometimes change in profound ways when some of these dynamics become visible. This kind of awareness was the hallmark of much of the best early "diversity" work. However, it was not enough to create clarity about what to do. Paradoxically, the best awareness was about big issues that were hard to connect to in an actionable way at the individual level. The second step of the SET model is the inflection point for real, granular change. *Engage System 2,* ES2, is the bridge from awareness to action.

Your System 2

Before we explain ES2, consider the following example. One of our consultants really likes to use this simple math problem to highlight System 2 thinking: A bat and a ball together cost $1.10. The bat costs $1.00 more than the ball. How much does the ball cost?

Quickly, what is your answer? Did you answer ten cents? If you did, then you are with the majority of those who have answered this problem. Like them, you are wrong. Before you start to engage System 2, we will tell you the answer is five cents. When presented with simple problems, we often come to quick solutions based on our prior experience. Malcolm Gladwell would call this "thin slicing." When we have enough experience, thin slicing can be very helpful and accurate. Your automatic decision-making cycle, also known as System 1, saw a simple math problem of $1.10 minus $1.00. Perhaps you did not focus on the words "more than" the ball or you came to the answer without going back to prove its correctness. In order for the bat and ball to cost a total of $1.10, when we know the bat was $1.00 more than the ball, the answer had to be between zero and ten cents for the cost of the ball. We could go one digit at a time from $1.01 to $1.02 to $1.03 and so on until we get the right answer, but to our lazier System 1 mind that is too much effort, so a quick decision without verification is given.

Psychologists have long used Systems 1 and 2 as explanations of how we make decisions. Daniel Kahneman, a Nobel Prize winner for economics, made these two systems popular to the layperson in his book *Thinking Fast and Slow* (a great read if you have the time). As you may have guessed from the above problem, System 2 involves more reflective decision making that requires a greater amount of energy and concentration. Since it involves this additional input, we only engage it when we are presented with challenges that we have consciously realized require more than a quick decision. For those of us who commute by car to work on a regular basis, it is not uncommon for our System 1 brain to take control of the wheel. Proof of this would be those times we drive home from work and then wonder how we got there without much recollection of any stoplight or intersection. We were driving in automatic mode. This is quite common and can be dangerous when we are distracted by such things as texting on our mobiles.

Now think about when summer comes and road construction begins. All of a sudden your normal path from work to home is blocked with detours. You are presented with a challenge. If you are on the phone, perhaps you tell the person to hold on as you figure out what you need to do. System 2 thinking requires concentration. If we tried to engage System 2 for every decision we make, we would never get out of bed. Life would be mentally exhausting. Also, constant System 2 thinking would be detrimental in situations in which we have to make quick, instinctive decisions, such as swerving when a child runs in front of the car. Think about this in the context of your everyday work environment. You get up to go to the cafeteria. In System 1 mode, you quickly say hello to or chat with the people you know best, the ones you have the most in common with—the ones most like you. You are sitting in your office one afternoon pondering a difficult problem, and you know you need another perspective. Who pops into your mind first? You have an opportunity to put one of your team in front of a top executive or a key client. Who do you choose? The safe System 1 choice is the person you perhaps know best, is most like you, and whose behavior you can most easily anticipate. System 1 will perpetuate sameness. Engaging System 2 will help you to break the status quo. In fact, ES2 is required to break the status quo in the day-to-day workplace dynamics. Shifting the status quo is what ES2 is all about. This is the fundamental work of creating inclusion.

Think about ES2 as the interrupter. Our brain much prefers System 1 thinking; it is easier and takes less energy. We unconsciously almost always prefer System 1 thinking. This is why unconscious bias is so powerful. Our brain takes predetermined and unexamined assumptions about groups of people and actually encourages us to make lots of little decisions based upon those assumptions; again, much of this is unconscious. Insider–outsider dynamics are often "baked into the cake"; they are implicit dynamics that can only be interrupted if we engage System 2. Basically, our physiology reinforces unintended bias, and this is why ES2 is so important. We have to create conscious intentional interrupters to minimize the impact of unconscious bias and insider–outsider dynamics. It doesn't matter how much profound awareness we have. It doesn't matter how inclusive our intent is. If we don't find practical, simple ways to force ourselves to engage our conscious brain, we simply won't achieve any real change and our good intent will not have the desired impact.

Self-awareness is arguably an interrupter all by itself. Any time we have increased self-awareness we are by definition interrupting our thought process. Think of your "aha" moments as the start of an interruption. ES2, though, goes beyond this. When we engage System 2 we are actually forcing self-awareness in moments that are important, when we know we might not have conscious awareness. We are proactively assuming that we will miss important moments and we are finding ways to force ourselves into our System 2 conscious brain.

The learning objective of any good leadership development is to understand when and how to engage System 2. This is what Jameson, Libby, and Mai are starting to do.

When to Engage System 2

As you may recall, Libby recently recruited two college hires. The lifeblood of the company is its campus recruitment program, and considerable investment is made planning, implementing, and carrying out the recruitment effort. Libby was very happy to have picked candidates she viewed as highly qualified. She knew strong hires make a stronger team. Libby did her market research on untapped opportunities in her region. It became clear that the growing Chinese American segment was not fully represented in the company's consumer targets, but it was also underleveraged by the competition. Low competition and low penetration create an opportunity for a huge win. Libby saw a simple problem (not unlike our earlier math problem): Which rep should she match with this market? Assigning Mai to this market didn't even warrant a second thought. In Libby's mind, she matched like with like. Mai, an Asian American, was matched with an Asian American market segment. Simple enough. However, from Chandler's point of view, he was not even considered for a potentially big win simply because of his ethnic background. Libby had the best of intentions. The assignment was a great opportunity for her new hire Mai, and Libby saw Mai as a good match for the market. That was System 1 thinking.

What about Jameson? Where was System 1 thinking coming to play in his decision making? There is a bit of a dichotomy that goes with experience. The more successful experiences we have, the likelier we are to rely on our gut instincts and the less likely we are to engage System 2 thinking. Our brains basically tell us that what we have done in the past made us successful, so let's stick to the plan. This path does help in a static environment. For example, relying on mutual fund managers was once key to financial success. However, the market and those who interact with the market do not retain the status quo for long, and a mutual fund manager alone no longer assures a good chance of success in this arena. Incredibly fast computers paired with highly sophisticated software now spot and exploit trends in a matter of seconds. Matching mutual fund managers with the new technology now offers the best chance at a winning hand.

Back to Jameson. His management team at All Vector helped lead the company to success. Why would he even think of changing that team after the merger with Strong Choice Investments? That his management team ended up being very similar to him in so many ways was just happenstance. Jameson believed there was a meritocracy in place and that everyone on his team deserved his position and rewards. He could point to each and every success his executives had achieved in order to get to that level. This thought process trickled down to the reorganization of offices. In each decision where an office had to be cut for market redundancy, All Vector offices won over SCI offices. Simple math only required System 1 automatic decision making.

All Vector was in status quo mode until it was not. Merging with SCI brought in new lines of business and a contrasting culture. The historical corporate challenges were no longer status quo. SCI built its success on working across differences. As a company, it penetrated markets where its competition had failed. Management had integrated diversity and inclusion leadership skill development into their core training from new hire orientation to client engagement. Whereas Jameson saw strength in his team's commonalities, SCI found excellence by leveraging difference.

When Jameson felt external pressure to make a showing

of diversity, System 1 thinking clicked in again; he decided to find a woman to promote to a senior role to prove that the company was inclusive. Again, the decision to simply respond to the bad press by hiring a token woman did not even enter into a discussion until he received some unexpected feedback from his family, as noted in the previous chapter. Just a few weeks into this heralded merger, and he has already had to take pause.

"It is not only management who has to stop and think," Mai thought out loud as she encountered her System 2 challenges. As an individual contributor, she was used to being given the path and told when to take it. Her initial foray into the market did not prove successful, even though she had followed the sales strategy step by step. All Vector had a proven sales strategy in which every rep was indoctrinated. She'd heard more stories of success than she could remember from the reps she encountered during her recruitment process. It was all very motivational. She was a dedicated learner and noted to be at the top of her class by the sales trainer. Therefore, Mai's lack of success could have been due to only one reason: the newly assigned market. There is a reason this market is not being won by anyone, she thought. Week after week she had no success stories to share at the team meetings, which made her retreat even more from interactions with others on the team. She felt a bit embarrassed by her tallies on the sales board. She was not of Chinese descent, and thus could not sell to that market any better than Chandler, she told herself.

Mai was falling into the same System 1 thinking that Libby employed when she assigned Mai to the market in the first place. Mai made a few quick assumptions: Libby did not understand the difference between Vietnamese and Chinese; her assigned market had no potential because it had no history of success; and All Vector sales training would work perfectly in all markets. Her conclusion was that there was nothing she could do except change territories. Again, this is a System 1 thought not requiring much reflection. When Mai asked Libby to discuss the market, Libby was deep in her preparation for her meeting with Jameson. Before Mai could give her reasons for requesting the change, Libby asked Mai to try the market for one more month. They agreed to schedule a meeting in one month's time to discuss territory assignments.

How to Engage System 2

Now let's go back to the workshop to see how all three were able to think about their specific challenges differently. Our colleagues have just been introduced to the subject of Systems 1 and 2 through some interactive discussion and practical examples. They were redirected to the list of decisions they brainstormed earlier in the workshop (the little day-to-day, moment-to-moment behaviors that impact people and may reflect unintended biases) and asked to pick three that were either common or critical for them personally and that, though small, have a significant impact on the people on their teams.

Before our three colleagues would be able to analyze their decisions, they had to work on when and how to engage System 2. As noted earlier, if you reflect deeply on every decision, you will be overwhelmed in a short period of time. System 1 automatic decision making is our default and is the easiest mode to engage. It is quite accurate for many of our daily decisions. The strategy we use in our workshops helps participants learn to predetermine when and how to engage System 2. The saying, "If you fail to plan, then you plan to fail" applies here.

Because System 1 thinking is so powerful and pervasive, we have to force our brains into System 2. We call this push a "System 2 moment." System 2 moments do not need to take a lot of time or be very complicated, they just need to connect to the decision points that are most impactful in the staff's ability to be fully engaged, included, and successful.

The focus should be on decisions that are both critical and routine. The most important consideration is whether the decision has an impact on people's ability to be successful. This can include critical decisions such as promotions and hiring, which are systemic in nature and will require a more systemic ES2 interrupter. However, smaller day-to-day decisions are at least as impactful—the ones that might seem innocuous when taken individually but can accumulate to have a real impact. The second consideration concerns the possibility of unconscious bias impacting the decision. Many people-related decisions have the potential to reflect unconscious bias, whether the decision regards who is or is not in line for promotion, who to bring to a key client meeting, or who to chat with for ten minutes over coffee. Any of these decisions—which are impactful and can reflect unconscious bias—is ripe for an ES2 moment.

For example, a norm can be established that one qualified individual who may not fit the typical profile be added to the pool. We call this the "Rule of One Uncommon." This rule can be applied in both promotions and hiring. If you have always hired Ivy League graduates, look to consider one qualified individual who graduated from an online university or a community college. The key words here are "qualified" and "consider." Your qualifications need to be a little less strict—that is, you could accept "a bachelor's degree" as the qualification instead of "a bachelor's degree from an Ivy League university." One of our insurance clients found that they were having a difficult time recruiting a diverse group of individuals. After some investigation we discovered they were looking only for candidates who had an insurance background, though it was not required to do the job. What the company really wanted was bright and well-connected individuals. When the recruitment team employed the Rule of One Uncommon, they started to consider firefighters, teachers, and police officers. None of these candidates had an insurance background, but all were well connected and respected figures in the community. After a few successful hires, they changed their recruitment profiles to be broader. More diverse candidates ended up greatly increasing revenue.

In some ways, it is easier to apply ES2 to these large systemic decisions than to the little day-to-day decisions. Now, you are probably scratching your head because we mentioned earlier that you cannot reflect on every decision, and yet we just said to apply ES2 to routine decisions. The caveat is that you should schedule time to go back and measure the effectiveness of the small decisions, rather than engaging System 2 for each routine decision in the moment. Perhaps you have a routine for conducting your weekly team meetings or engaging a client for the first time. Put a reminder in your calendar three months out to measure the effectiveness of the decisions you made. When we measure effectiveness or analyze results, we are purposefully engaging our System 2 mind. Set aside a time and place where distractions will be minimal. If the routine decision is meeting your objective, set another calendar reminder six to twelve months out to do another check. Seldom do our environments remain static, so we need to create purposeful check-ins to stay on top of changes.

Typical routine decisions for which we often do not engage System 2 thinking include those small relationship-building moments. Affinity bias, our tendency to interact with those we share commonalities with, often comes into to play and creates an uneven relationship-building playing field. It is far too easy to have regular discussions with the same person every day. Maybe you share an interest in soccer with someone on your team; every day you have a few minutes of small talk around this topic. Little by little, you start to develop a casual and easy relationship with this teammate. When it comes time to make a quick project assignment, you choose him because of this relationship influence. All the while, you do not share any obvious interests with two other people on your team, so those daily moments do not happen and those relationships are not strengthened.

Your ES2 strategy should focus on the multiple levels of system we discussed in chapter 1. Consider applying System 2 moments at the individual interpersonal level, with a focus on relationships and interactions; at the group and team level, with a focus on team dynamics; at the organizational level, with a focus on talent acquisition and talent management processes; and at the marketplace level, with a focus on client development.

The first part of your ES2 strategy should be to determine if you've been building relationships in an inequitable manner. To get started, consider keeping a small diary that notes the people you spend your time with and the amount of time you spent with each. As with a diet diary that notes everything you eat, your log will likely show that the small items add up. If you have a couple minutes of conversation with Paul or Marsha on your way to your office, jot it down. If somebody pops her head in the door for a five-minute meeting or schedules a sixty-minute meeting, make a note. After a month or two, you will be able to graph your time with everybody on your team. Don't forget to keep track of any individuals you manage remotely. If you are client facing, this approach is also handy for determining client relationship moments. Our human tendency to gravitate toward those who are similar to us extends to our client relationships.

The same strategy can apply to many talent development activities. Make a list of project or client assignments. Give each a grade, 1 being low profile, 2 neutral, and 3 high profile. Now list the primary person assigned to each project. Take notice if one person is given more opportunity than others. Also, take note of group dynamics. For example, are all of the high-profile assignments going to people in one particular age group or gender? Challenge yourself on the assignments. Although you cannot engage System 2 for every decision, decisions involving relationship building and talent development opportunities have what we call an accumulation effect. Normally, D&I does not enter the conversation until the final decision about who to promote or hire is pending, if D&I is raised at all. However, all of the little moment-by-moment interactions accumulate to impact performance and heavily influence that end decision.

You can even track talent acquisition activities. If you are involved in campus recruiting, track the demographic profile of the students you approach and those who approach you. If you are involved in interviewing, include in your notes a section on informal interaction. For example, you can record how much time you spent chatting versus time in the formal part of the interview. Start to talk about these data points in the selection meeting.

The act of tracking this data is an ES2 strategy, one that bridges awareness and interruption. Just the act of forcing yourself to gather the data interrupts the automatic System 1 thought process; raising your awareness around any inequitable situation almost always helps to create a correction. Again, the diet analogy works well here. In the August 2008 edition of the *American Journal of Medicine* is a study on keeping a diet journal. Subjects who were asked to simply write down everything they ate lost weight because they raised their awareness of their food intake. They then self-corrected on all of the small items that had an accumulation effect. Dr. Victor Stevens, senior investigator at the Kaiser Permanente Center for Health Research, noted that the most powerful predictor for weight loss was how many days a week the study participants were faithful to journaling their diet.

An accumulation effect can also impact innovation and teaming. Innovation is all about getting out of our System 1 thinking. Often, we will systematize innovation based upon our own set of experiences and abilities. If we have always experienced innovation events via brainstorming meetings, then that will most likely be the go-to process when we lead efforts for innovation. However, if we were not exposed to difference along the way, we may not be aware of how innovation can be spurred from various types of activities. Those who are extraverted may work well with high-energy brainstorming team events. Introverts may prefer more time to think on their own, and will perhaps perform better via an anonymous collaborative site. Try different forms of innovation to create a more inclusive dynamic. Every team has a set of norms, and these often operate without our being conscious of them. As a team leader, you can create System 2 moments by varying the pace, the location, and the leadership of meetings. One of our clients had a very successful outcome by rotating the leadership of his biweekly team meetings so that a different team member led each one. He included remote locations as well, creating a much higher level of engagement and visibility of remote staff. If he hadn't done this, the team would have continued the dynamic of predictable team meetings with the highest participation coming from the same people, mostly in the central corporate location. He told us that not only was he noticing much higher levels of participation, he was also able to better assess the leadership and intangible skills of more of his team, and he was pleasantly surprised. All of that from one simple System 2 moment.

Their Three Decisions

Jameson wrote down the three decisions he thought were important to focus on. Libby did the same. The group was then paired off. Each pair was to explain the decisions they chose and why. Jameson and Libby ended up paired together.

Jameson took the liberty of sharing his decisions first. He had picked promotions, recognition, and team assignments, and went on to explain that these are the people-related decisions that are typically on his desk. Since turnover on Jameson's team was almost nonexistent, his direct hiring was extremely minimal. It was Libby's role as the other part of that pair to challenge Jameson's choice. She acknowledged that having inclusion at the forefront in those choices was important, but wondered if the decision was already made by the time the choice was before him. Jameson asked what she meant. She asked Jameson candidly whether, if a SVP position were to open up now, he already knew who he would want to fill it. He nodded in the affirmative.

Libby reminded Jameson of the accumulation effect that had been discussed earlier in the workshop. She asked him if there are smaller decisions that have a big influence on promotions, recognition, or team assignments. Jameson admitted that those individuals who were top of mind for any reward were typically those he had the most exposure to. He then scratched promotions and recognition off his list and replaced them with informal social time and mentoring. These two decisions, along with team assignments, seemed to be a much better fit.

Libby shared her decisions. She chose meeting norms, employee time, and rewards. As the challenger, Jameson asked Libby to be more precise. All three of those decisions seemed a bit hard to measure. Libby explained that she wanted to make sure inclusion was part of all of those decisions, but when Jameson reminded her that she cannot engage System 2 in every situation, she agreed that in order to gain traction she would need to be more specific. They hashed out which decisions had a higher impact than others. They decided that meeting norms should be specified and decided she should evaluate whom she chose to lead meetings and when the meetings should be scheduled. For employee time, Libby knew the client "ride-alongs" were the most useful, as they provided her a chance to see staff in action as well as ample time for feedback and relationship building. For rewards, she thought the single biggest reward was deciding on market/client assignments. All three were specific, measureable, and easy to implement.

Meanwhile, in the workshop for the client-facing team, Mai was making a list of her own decisions. She had come into this workshop not truly understanding what she could do to create a more inclusive workplace. After all, she did not have D&I in her list of job responsibilities and she did not manage people. Initially, she thought she and her fellow reps, as well as the executives in their workshop, were all there as part of some type of compliance policy so everyone could check the box. However, from the very start, the conversation was connected not only to her colleagues but also to her client base. When she thought about it, she was managing her clients in much the same way her leader was managing the team. Though the goals were different, it was nonetheless people management. From all of the market-leading research, she knew VeStrong's target clientele was increasingly more diverse. In the consumer market, women—who were once the minority in financial decision making—were trending toward being the primary decision makers. In the June 2014 Ameriprise Financial survey

"Women and Financial Power," 56 percent of women said they share in making financial decisions with their spouses while 41 percent said they are making financial decisions on their own. As VeStrong eyed global markets, it was only too clear they would need to work across differences effectively or risk losing market share.

The facilitator asked reps to have at least one decision focused on their internal team and one on the market. With the help of her partner, Mai was able to write down three clear, measureable decisions. Although Mai tended to be a loner in the office, she knew she had to consider her social event decisions, the ones about whether to lunch alone or with colleagues and whether to attend after-work events. Most colleagues were out visiting clients during the day, so those social events were key to relationship building. On the client side, Mai thought she should consider who and how she usually engages first for business. She could easily create a spreadsheet of titles and methods to engage, such as phone, drop-by visits, or group events. As a data-centric person, she found the third decision area easy to determine. She was going to focus on her decision about where to derive market data. She knew the vast majority of her data was being derived from the Internet instead of in person.

Multiple Learning Moments

The purpose of the decision exercise is twofold. First, the participants take time to think about the decisions, routine or critical, that may have an impact on inclusivity, regardless of their intent. The corporate world ties rewards with impact. You may have had the best of intentions to beat analyst forecasts, but unless you actually do it, you are not rewarded with a higher stock valuation. By explicitly engaging System 2 on the impact of their people-related decisions, participants can skip past the conversation around intent as we assume good intent is foundational to anyone wanting a successful team. The second purpose is to gain practice in challenging decisions around inclusion, even well-intended decisions. The challenger engages System 2 from the other side of the table by inquiring about the decision-maker's assumptions or unintentional biases.

You will notice the first part of "Engage System 2" was tracking and measuring, or raising consciousness of behaviors. In order to understand whether the proverbial playing field is tilted, employees need to first find a way to measure their behavior and then to determine if it is having an inequitable impact. Accurate discernment requires looking at a lot of small behaviors and how they add up—the accumulation effect. There are many decisions in the typical work life of every employee, whether she is a manager or an individual contributor, that impact or involve people. From this long list of decisions, the employee needs to choose a few key ones to focus on. Research has shown that if you focus on making just a couple of improvements instead of trying to accomplish a lengthy laundry list of changes, you are far more likely to implement change.

Speaking of change, in the next chapter we will focus on action plans. Although all three of our colleagues were experiencing those "aha" moments in the workshop, they will not see a return unless they can transform those insights into action. Jameson began to understand that inclusion is not something to consider in only the critical decisions such as promotions or team assignments. Libby got a better understanding of how to focus her plans on more specific, measureable actions. Mai gained the insight that inclusion is not only something everybody in the company should own from entry level to the C-suite, it also plays a critical role in client engagement. All three were envisioning diversity and inclusion as a concept that went beyond HR and was truly connected to the success of the business.

Before we can get to action plans, though, we need to consider not only our targeted behaviors but also what success metrics we will use. As part of the sales team, Mai had access to all her client data, which could be easily be tracked. The connection with her colleagues was going to be a little more difficult. She chose to simply measure it by the number of interactions she had.

Libby planned to ask her assistant to help keep her honest with regard to her actions. Her assistant could keep a running tally on how she was performing with regard to the three decisions she had highlighted. Jameson took Libby's lead with this approach, but he also wanted to measure the impact the workshops had on the entire team. He'd recently sat in on a demo of a software that tracks HRIS demographics and pairs it up with actions such as hires, promotions, raises, and development opportunities. It is an enterprise-wide tool that allows real-time analysis of the organization's diversity and inclusion goal attainment as well as measuring the individual impact of everyone who attended the workshop.

After an engaging discussion around their decisions and ways to measure the success of any actions, they were all set (excuse the pun) to move on to the "Tailor" step of the SET model.

Key Takeaways

- ✓ You cannot engage System 2 for every decision or you will be overwhelmed.
- ✓ Leverage self-awareness to determine the highest-priority areas in which you should engage System 2.
- ✓ Inclusion works both internally and externally.
- ✓ To exact lasting change, go beyond individual behaviors and consider systemic written and unwritten norms.

3

Tailor

The person who says it cannot be done should
not interrupt the person doing it.
—*Chinese proverb*

In the introduction, we highlighted our three colleagues Jameson, Libby, and Mai, and we gave you some context surrounding their inclusion challenges. In the setup, Libby suggested, and Jameson approved, a pilot workshop focused on unconscious bias and inclusive leadership development. Initially, the reason for the pilot was a large RFP that requested detailed information on VeStrong's diversity and inclusion efforts. However, Jameson and Libby quickly realized they were getting a lot more out of the workshop than they had anticipated. Mai, as an individual contributor, was quite surprised by the part she played in creating an inclusive culture. She had long thought that D&I was solely the role of the largely white male leadership, and not something for which she shared any responsibility. As Mai went through the portion of the workshop on step 1, Self-Awareness, she saw connections to her teammates and her clients. The Engage System 2 section allowed her to stop and analyze inclusion dynamics from an entirely different angle. Mai was happy she'd been invited to participate in the workshop, as she saw it contributing to her future success.

All three colleagues were earnestly invested in carrying the workshop learnings forward and realizing an inclusion dividend. Since the "Tailor" step is all about changing behavior based on self-awareness and engaging System 2, you may be surprised to realize it is the shortest segment of the workshop. However, it is actually the longest-lived part of the development. The workshop segment is short because much of the heavy introspective work had already been done; this piece of the puzzle is about setting up a plan to put everything into action. Actions are taken in the participants' real lives, not in the workshop. Although some participants start scheduling time on their calendar to carry out the action steps before they leave the workshop, the real work is completed the moment everyone leaves the room.

We will review each of our colleagues' committed action plans and then their actual implementation. Remember, the goal of the workshop was not to just produce aha moments, but rather to create sustainable change. Sustainable change is measured in short- and long-term goals. Some inclusion goals, such as developing a more diverse pipeline for management positions, may take years to measure, while other goals, such as enabling fuller team engagement, can be realized in months.

Libby's Action Plan Implementation

Libby is first on our list, as she has the most challenging situation of the three. As a middle manager, Libby needs to consider the sales teams she manages directly, her own peers in sales management, and the executive management above her. As CEO, Jameson's focus is on his direct reports and the organizational impact. On the other end of the org structure is Mai, who does not have anybody reporting to her, but who does need to manage her team and management interactions. All three have client influences, however Mai has the most daily client interaction.

In the workshop, Libby decided to create action plans around meeting norms, market/client assignments, and time spent with reports (more specifically, ride-alongs). First up, meeting norms. On the subject of meeting norms, she had three simple actions she knew she could accomplish in fairly short order. One idea she had was to institute a rotating meeting lead position. Each monthly meeting will start with a fifteen-minute presentation by a different member of the team. In an e-mail, she let her team know that the leader for the month would choose a subject he believed to be of value to the group. She initially asked for volunteers to lead the next meeting, but discovered that only those individuals who had always been team leaders offered to volunteer (Self-Awareness). She stopped to reflect (Engage

System 2) and determined that she had established a pattern of expectation in the group around who was counted on to lead and who was not. She tailored the action in the moment and let her team know that she was going to rotate alphabetically based on last name.

The next meeting was in three weeks, so everyone had plenty of time to prepare. Libby asked the reps to send her their chosen topics so she could integrate them into her piece of the meeting. Mai was scheduled to lead the meeting after next, and sent along the topic of Asian American market targeting. Libby was halfway through a reply to Mai asking her if that topic was of value to the entire team, since none them had a heavy focus on this market, when she stopped herself. A few questions popped into Libby's head as she paused in drafting her e-mail. Why do I think this market would not be of interest to the other team members? Couldn't everyone find value in demographic market targeting? She erased the e-mail and replied, "Thank you. Look forward to it." Just a month earlier, she would have automatically sent the e-mail and relegated the interest of demographic markets solely to those who had a membership in them. Today, she understood that there was value for the entire team in broadening their horizons for a more inclusive client approach.

Another meeting norm Libby knew she could easily change was the timing. She was having the meeting at 7 a.m. on Mondays. However, in her SVP position, her regional responsibilities were expanded across time zones. She'd also discovered in the workshop piece on insider–outsider dynamics that the company geared times for those without family responsibilities, often scheduling meetings early in the morning when kids had to be taken to school or day care. Another norm was having retreats on weekends, though many preferred to be with their loved ones on those days. The 7 a.m. Monday meeting had been scheduled for a valid reason, as it was held before client meeting times. Libby opted to rotate the meetings, holding them at 8 a.m., noon, and 5 p.m., and then measuring team engagement and attendance to determine the best fit.

The last meeting norm she was going to engage was the innovation section of the meeting, when she would typically have a call-out green-light forum. As with the meeting times, Libby decided the best approach would be a varied one. In the traditional meetings, there would always be a handful of individuals she could count on for good ideas. She knew that in order to stay competitive the entire team would need to be leveraged. She devised two other methods for innovation. First, she would alter the green-light session, creating bit of a delay by presenting the challenge in the meeting announcement and encouraging everyone to write in one innovative idea. The ideas were then presented anonymously to the group to discuss during the meeting. By presenting ideas anonymously, Libby hoped to curtail the team's bias toward certain individuals. The second method was to form online collaborative groups that would compete as collectives instead of individuals.

How did Libby's meeting change plans turn out? She found that there was no meeting time that would please everyone. The same went for the innovation meetings. Some team members, including her, had just gotten comfortable in their routines. Change was not always welcome. None of that was surprising. What was surprising was how those members she had written off had all of a sudden become strong contributors. She had three sales reps with young children who in the past either missed or were non-responsive in the morning meetings, but were now very active in the afternoon sessions. The introverts in her group who were wallflowers during the traditional innovation meetings had put forward some game-changing ideas when they were given more time and could contribute anonymously. Libby was conscious not to relegate the past performers to the back of the line. She discussed with the team the idea of rotating times and methods, and they all thought it was a good idea.

In addition to these inclusion bonuses, having a different team member lead a portion of the meeting allowed Libby and the team to get to know all the team members better, not just the handful who were most vocal. Her action item around team ride-alongs also allowed Libby more access to the entire team. In the past, it seemed as if those with the most access to Libby were the ones who were able to get her to come along to client meetings. Libby asked her assistant to make sure there was at least one person every week for a ride-along whom she had not accompanied in the past. What she discovered was enlightening. Being with someone in a car created a level of connection not possible in the office. But Libby found that spending quality time with her diverse staff was sometimes awkward, particularly when team members were different from her by race and ethnicity. She could see why it was so easy to stay in her comfort zone and spend the most time with the team members most like herself. However, over time, the awkwardness diminished and this had an exponential effect, improving the amount and quality of interaction back in the office. There was no replacement for developing a good rapport with her team.

An additional important and directly commercial benefit emerged from these ride-alongs. When she was joining the same successful individuals, she saw the company's sales approach working for their targeted traditional core clients. However, when she had diverse exposure to her sales reps, she started to realize the sales approach was not as successful in certain segments. Libby selected a group of sales reps and asked them to work with the sales trainer to modify the approach for a more successful outcome in different segments.

Mai's Action Plan Implementation

Mai noted that Libby was taking all of the workshop learnings to heart, which meant a lot to her. Libby had really been trying to make a genuine personal connection, and it was making Mai feel more relaxed and engaged. So often, leaders would go through development, yet nothing would change. The training would be just another flavor-of-the-month effort, and sales reps would hold their breath and wait for it to pass. After this workshop, though, Mai could see a marked difference in the way the team was reacting to Libby. At first they were skeptical of the suggestions, but once they realized they were more of a long-term behavioral change, they got on board. Although Mai had a lot of good intentions when she left the workshop, she knew that if her leadership did not follow through it would make it very difficult for her to fully incorporate her workshop goals.

Mai had three action paths to pursue: team interaction, client engagement, and market prep work. Coming out of the unconscious bias workshop geared for individual contributors, Mai did not know the action plan Libby had created in the management session. However, it felt like the plans had been made in unison, as Libby's inclusion actions directly supported Mai's approach. When the timing of the monthly meetings changed, Mai had more exposure to a larger group of team members. Whereas Mai was fairly quiet during the traditional innovative sessions, which privileged the highly extroverted, mostly male team members, the mixed-team approach not only increased her interaction with colleagues but also her contributions to innovation.

All of Libby's efforts made Mai's action plan much easier to attain. Mai made a concerted effort to widen her social group beyond her comfortable circle of colleagues. Mai joined the African American employee resource group (ERG) as an ally member. Attending their events gave her insight into a group she had very little exposure to growing up. There were many common challenges shared among many of the employee resource groups related to their outsider group memberships.

In the past, Mai had shied away from joining the Asian American group, as she thought participating would reinforce treatment of her as a member of a group instead of as an individual. In the workshop, she realized that we are all simultaneously unique individuals and group members who share commonalities. Every person could embrace her group memberships while remaining a distinct individual. Joining the Asian American employee resource group allowed her to fulfill two of her action plans; it enlarged her circle of colleagues and gave her another source for market research. She quickly discovered the external network that could be tapped via the ERG. It was this ERG membership that gave her the idea to present on targeting demographic markets when it was her turn to lead the monthly meeting.

Mai's discussion first focused on the commonalities shared across markets, such as life events, that sparked the need for insurance or financial planning. Mai then shared how modifying the sales approach to be sensitive to cultural nuances allowed the sales rep to become a trusted financial advisor. She showed the team a very structured yet simple three-step process to modify their approach for their specific audience. Libby quickly recognized that Mai was using the SET approach to improve her market standing. The engagement with the team members, who commented on how this approach could be used for their target market, was surprisingly active. Every sales rep was able to take something from Mai's presentation to help him in his specific markets, even if those markets were not specifically focused on a cultural demographic. It also opened up Libby's eyes, as several sales reps shot off e-mails after the call asking her how they could be assigned an underserved market segment.

Chandler, the other college hire brought on with Mai, whom Libby never even gave a second thought when assigning the Asian American market, stopped by her office to inquire about the possibility of teaming up with Mai. He told Libby that his wife is Chinese American and he has quite a bit of knowledge of the cultural market. Chandler was impressed by Mai's approach and thought they could learn from each other. He had some early wins that could be shared with Mai as well. The request and further knowledge about Chandler reminded Libby of a workshop discussion around visible and invisible dimensions of difference. (More information on dimensions of difference can be found in *The Inclusion Dividend*.) She found herself often relying solely on diversity aspects she could immediately determine or reasonably guess, such as gender, ethnicity, and age. If one scratches the surface to see the less visible differences, there are many more dimensions of difference to be found, including our relationships (sexual orientation, marital status, etc.), parental status, veterans' status, and even many disabilities. All of these dimensions create the unique individuals we are.

All three of Mai's action plans were paying dividends quickly. The various team interactions, which seemed uncomfortable to her at the beginning, helped form a stronger internal support network. They also gave her access to external networks that enhanced her market penetration. This approach dovetailed with her effort to diversify her market prep work so that instead of relying solely on the Internet and data research, she was acquiring a higher percentage from in-person interviews and introductions. Both these action steps allowed Mai to engage her clients more fully.

Learning about insider–outsider dynamics from the workshop gave her insight into how some of these dynamics could be playing out in her client base. She found that connecting with clients based on their shared outsider groups formed a stronger bond of trust. In any market, trust was the common link that determined client success in financial services.

Jameson's Action Plan Implementation

Jameson understood that trust determined internal team success as well. As the CEO, he was entrusted with making the best decisions for company growth. His team also trusted him to support a fully meritocratic organization. When signs of favoritism showed, regardless of whether it was conscious or unconscious, that trust was eroded. The CEO was judged not only for his actions, but also for the actions of his management team. He bore the burden or applause for any organization-wide impact. As the company leader, Jameson is a model for other executives, who see his behavior (good or bad) as the standard. He wanted to make sure his actions had an impact beyond his immediate reports. He knew his actions would influence the organizational culture, so he could not appear to be simply checking off a box when it came to D&I or passing the responsibility along to other employees. He needed to embody the change.

The first action on Jameson's list was to diversify his informal social time. This social time encompassed the time outside of meetings during which he interacted with other employees. An easy step was to start attending some of the employee resource group events as a member and not as the occasional guest speaker. In the past, he had seen these events as duties that had him running in late to give a fifteen-minute talk and then heading out before the meeting was over. He now wanted to be part of the audience as a learning member. This would also allow him to socialize with a more diverse set of employees. The African American ERG was holding a forum on cultural marketing. Jameson sat down next to Mai, cocked his head inquisitively, and immediately wanted to ask her what she was doing there. His System 1 thinking quickly assessed she was not African American and he wondered why she attended. Before he engaged System 2, Mai introduced herself. She told Jameson she had attended the unconscious bias workshop and one of her action plans was to increase her exposure to more colleagues and build her knowledge of other cultures. Jameson smiled and said he was basically doing the same thing. After the meeting ended, Mai observed that much of what they'd discussed could be applied to her market segment. Jameson discovered Mai was one of Libby's college recruits and he thought that both Libby and Mai could benefit from his second action plan of shaking up his mentoring approach.

Jameson asked if Mai could schedule a meeting with the two of them and Libby to review a more formal mentorship. He told Mai it was to be a two-way mentoring. Jameson wanted her to provide him with insight into her market as well as into the overall frontline team culture. In return, he would share his experience and provide career counseling. Mai's direct insight into a market that had been coming up in various investor calls would prove to be a big benefit. Until now, Jameson had only received market reports for this data, which did not provide him the richer understanding of the market that Mai could offer.

Beyond attending the ERG events, Jameson thought about the small social interactions that he had previously thought were insignificant. He'd realized in the workshop that they had a cumulative effect, so he chose to walk a different floor at least once a week on his way into the office. Along the way, he met different teams and team members. He decided to ask each person he encountered two questions: "How am doing as your CEO?" and "What is one piece of advice you could give me to be a better leader?" At first, the employees were a bit dumbfounded, but by the time his repeated questions got around the organization the staff was ready and armed with answers. He was amazed by two things: first, the genuine positive impact the questions had upon team morale once the employees knew he was taking their answers to heart; and second, the myriad answers he was receiving. On corporate financial management, they thought he was excelling. On employee engagement, they perceived him as aloof and uncaring. The legacy team from Strong Choice Investments did not view him in an overall favorable light and regarded his actions as rife with favoritism. As for suggestions, there was resounding support for him continuing to venture outside his traditional circles with activities such as walking different floors.

By exposing himself to more of the organization, Jameson could see the diversity challenges in certain departments that had not been obvious on paper, or which had previously been confined to company reports. HR was almost all women. Conversely, IT was almost all men. Finance had a much older population compared to public relations. He was amazed by how much he was seeing now that he hadn't noticed before. Each group created a ghetto of likeness, which had Jameson thinking about the company's talent acquisition policies. The unconscious bias workshop touched upon how biases could get embedded at the systemic level, creating barriers to inclusion. He made a note for the recruitment team to attend an unconscious bias workshop focused on talent acquisition. He'd recently read a 2013 Federal Reserve Bank of New York staffing report that noted that over 63 percent of referrals were of the same sex and over 71 percent were of the same ethnicity as the individual who referred them.

After implementing his first two actions, on informal social interactions and mentoring, Jameson found his last action, on team assignments, to be tremendously easy. Before increasing his exposure to a larger group of individuals, he'd had a fairly small pool of people who were top of mind. Over the past few months, his world had expanded exponentially. Suddenly he discovered he had a much richer and more diverse group of people to consider when it came to team assignments. He also had expanded his traditional definition of "fit." The exposure increased his self-awareness, while engaging System 2 thinking for critical decisions allowed him to pause and consider other options. His company had long preached to its clients about diversifying their investment portfolios; Jameson was finally taking this advice to his team and seeing the payout potential. There was one barrier, though, that he was starting to bump into.

The Organizational Impact

In the last large talent review meeting, at which he and his direct reports look two, and sometimes three, levels deep to identify top talent, he mentioned that there was not a lot of diversity in the pool of "high potentials." Some on his team looked uncomfortable. One remarked that it was important to promote people based on performance, and that there should be a meritocracy. Jameson remembered his daughter mentioning that the last thing she would want would be to get promoted because she is a woman. He didn't want his new focus on D&I to be perceived as a quota system, but it made no sense that the best-performing talent was such a non-diverse profile. He knew this gap was related to unconscious bias and insider–outsider dynamics. He also knew that it couldn't be fixed easily. He would not set people up to fail. He issued a challenge to his team; they would each have to identify and begin to mentor two individuals who were different from themselves. He told them he has already started that process by mentoring a high-potential Asian American female sales rep. He realized talent management was going to be a tough nut to crack, and he would need to develop a clear action plan that involved his entire leadership team.

A side benefit to all of Jameson's actions was the change in management's behavior. Knowing that Jameson was making the extra effort to be more inclusive, the management team naturally mirrored his actions. The team increasingly became more engaged at every level. The new approach was even translating to the marketplace: clients were more engaged, and thus retention increased and service penetration grew. Jameson personally got involved in the reissued RFP that had requested more D&I data. In the company's response, Jameson wrote a personal letter to the client CEO candidly noting that VeStrong had not achieved the D&I goals the company sought, but is making strides to create a more inclusive culture. He invited the client to attend one of VeStrong's workshops and to partner with the company on some inclusion initiatives. A day after the client received the response, the CEO called Jameson directly and had a thirty-minute conversation solely on D&I. He too was "behind the eight ball" when it came to developing a truer meritocracy and was thankful that Jameson was honest and open to partnership. One week later, VeStrong was delivered one of its largest wins.

Jameson realized that, although his organization had a great service to offer, clients expected a great deal of added value in a competitive market. VeStrong saw its vendor–partner relationships improve, with greater innovation and service, when the commitment to diversity was robust.

All three of our colleagues derived a dividend from their commitment to following through with their inclusive action plans. Some behavioral changes were a bit uncomfortable at first—Jameson walking the different floors, Libby sharing control of her meetings, or Mai attending employee resource group meetings. However, they were all pleasantly surprised at both the short-term benefit of exposing themselves to new ideas and the long-term payout of increased trust and an expanded network. As stated at the beginning of this chapter, "Tailor" is the shortest segment of the workshop but it is the longest endeavor because it requires the long-term fulfillment of your action plans. Developing actions that are practical, immediately implementable, and have a high impact on long-term relations are key to the success of the SET methodology.

Key Takeaways

✓ Initial actions need to be practical and easily implemented.

- ✓ Culture sustainment is measured on short- and long-term goals.
- ✓ A good action plan is dynamic; any action, whether it is successful or not, will result in learning and new actions.
- ✓ Leadership action has a higher impact on corporate culture because of its visibility.
- ✓ Action plans at different levels of leadership support one another in the greater scheme.
- ✓ Tailoring your behavior and your organization's approach to D&I is a long-term project that requires support at all levels.

Conclusion

Leadership should be born out of the
understanding of the needs of those
who would be affected by it.
—*Marian Anderson*

It is far too easy to say it is too hard to make a difference when you have been to diversity and inclusion workshops with the best of intent and great instruction, but have found limited or no movement in the culture. The simple and straightforward SET methodology was created to help move participants from awareness to action. SET provides a memorable approach that you can leverage outside the development environment.

Jameson, Libby, and Mai all had their own unique set of challenges and experiences. They shared a common good intent, which was being thwarted by unintended biases. All three were focused on success for themselves and their teams, and they assumed good intent was sufficient. Their external world perceived the matter differently; impact mattered more than intent. The press, clientele, and investors saw an acquisition of a diverse company by a firm that was not valuing diversity. Jameson thought he was managing the new organization for success, but he quickly became embroiled in a battle of perception that could have spun out of control and had a negative marketplace impact.

Jameson's "aha" moment (self-awareness) came when he took stock of the lack of diversity in his network and realized how he was unintentionally limiting his exposure to difference, which led to groupthink. By engaging System 2 thinking, he was able to stop and reflect on some of his everyday decisions that were having a cumulative effect on the larger people-related decisions such as hiring, promotions, or assignments. He had not kept up with the way D&I had moved from compliance to a market differentiator. Once he made himself aware of this point, he realized the overwhelming interest of clientele. In one quick survey, Jameson found that over 40 percent of their requests for proposal were asking for detail on the company's D&I initiatives. Furthermore, of those RFPs that did require D&I data, prior to the workshop his team was losing them at almost double the rate when compared to those RFPs that did not ask. But the workshop yielded results beyond the numbers: once Jameson started implementing his "Tailor" action plan, he found himself more engaged. His network expanded beyond the boardroom. The energy he felt from the organization improved markedly. As he helped create a more inclusive environment, he felt more included as well. Work was, well, feeling a lot less like work.

For too long, work had felt just like work for Libby. Not only did she feel she had to put in extra effort in order to be rewarded at the same level as her male peers, she also needed to expend energy on compartmentalizing the times (tucking these feelings away) she did not feel like an equal social member of the team. Arguably one of All Vector's best employees, Libby already had one foot out the door when news of the acquisition was announced. Although she was seeking a more inclusive culture, she was unconsciously building an uneven playing field for her own team. In the workshop, her self-awareness moment came when she noticed that most people view insider–outsider groups only when they are members of the outsider group. Because of her own insider group memberships, Libby did not think twice about the issues of outsider groups, which is why she automatically assigned Mai to the Chinese American market segment. Libby also realized she was building a team that relied on a couple of individuals she favored. Her choice of who to spend time with and how to manage meetings reinforced her confirmation biases. Once she'd engaged a more reflective System 2 thought process on these actions and their outcomes, she was taken aback that she was re-creating a culture like the one she was trying to leave. Although tailoring her actions was, at first, uncomfortable, her new approach provided welcome perspectives. Her team, which once had only a couple of star players, blossomed into a team of all-stars envied by other managers. Furthermore, her actions paved the way for others, including Mai, to implement their inclusive efforts.

Mai had long held onto to the belief that diversity and inclusion were the responsibility of management. Although Mai was new to the workforce, her academic viewpoint of diversity was something that was solely connected to diversity talent acquisition goals. It was not until she'd expanded her view during the self-awareness portion of the workshop that she understood the larger picture. By engaging System 2 for her interactions with her colleagues and clients, she quickly discovered a host of dividends from developing an inclusive approach to her clients and teammates.

In coordination with Libby's efforts, Mai tailored an action plan that increased her collegial exposure, enhanced her client network, and, most importantly, generated a genuine team feeling. When she made the effort to hear other people's voices, her own voice was increasingly heard.

The SET model gave all three colleagues the ability to leverage inclusive concepts, which can sometimes feel complex, into easily implemented practical actions that made a difference. Their impact was eventually large and systemic, although it started as an effort that was small, specific, and granular. We believe that is the trick to creating real and sustainable inclusion. An organization needs to have great and innovative diversity policies and practices, but these only have maximum impact when individual leaders change their day-to-day behavior. In today's extremely frantic work environment, where it seems like everything is a priority, leaders need a straightforward method for matching their intent with their impact. They do not walk out of a workshop the most inclusive leaders, but they do walk out with a plan to immediately set out on that path.

As we stated at the beginning of the book, our characters were fabricated by piecing together observations from our twenty-plus years of experience in this field. We hope their stories resonated with you whether you are in the C-suite, middle management, or just starting as an individual contributor. If you have attended a SET for Inclusion workshop and would like to share your success stories or just want to learn more, please e-mail us at Info@TheDagobaGroup.com. We are all on this journey together.

Index